333.79
MET

Nuclear Power

Other books in the Fueling the Future series:

Nuclear Power

Tom and Gena Metcalf, *Book Editors*

Christine Nasso, *Publisher*
Elizabeth Des Chenes, *Managing Editor*

GREENHAVEN PRESS

An imprint of Thomson Gale, a part of The Thomson Corporation

Detroit • New York • San Francisco • New Haven, Conn. • Waterville, Maine • London

Picture Credits:
Cover: © Royalty free/CORBIS; AP Photo/Issac Becken, 85; AP Photo/Fluor Daniel, 83; AP Photo/U.S. Department of Energy, 82; Associated Press, AP, 26; © Bettmann/CORBIS, 11, 13, 20, 24, 29, 53, 65; © Bohemian Nomad Picturemakers/CORBIS, 109; © Lowell Georgia/CORBIS, 87, 92; © Richard Hamilton-Smith/CORBIS, 85; © Hulton-Deutsch Collection/CORBIS, 40; © Igor Kostin/CORBIS, 43; © Dan Lamount/CORBIS, 74, 79; © Reuters/CORBIS, 37, 57; © Roger Ressmeyer/CORBIS, 60, 71, 73, 75, 81; © Royalty Free/CORBIS, 95, 98, 100; © Tim Wright/CORBIS, 66; © CORBIS, 18, 21; Getty Images, 33; Hulton Archive/Getty Images, 16; Time Life Pictures/Getty Images, 35; Santi Burgos/Bloomberg News/Landov, 54; dpa/Landov, 44; Rahed Homavandi/Reuters/Landov, 110; Frank Polich/Reuters/Landov, 68; Steve Zmina, 27, 47, 49, 50, 88, 91, 104

LIBRARY OF CONGRESS CATALOGING-IN-PUBLICATION DATA
Nuclear power / Tom and Gena Metcalf, book editors.

    p. cm. — (Fueling the future)
      Includes bibliographical references and index.
      ISBN 13: 978-0-7377-3587-1 (hardcover : alk. paper)
      ISBN 10: 0-7377-3587-2 (hardcover : alk. paper)
    1. Nuclear engineering—Juvenile literature. 2. Nuclear energy—Juvenile literature.
I. Metcalf, Tom. II. Metcalf, Gena.
  TK9148.N83 2006
  333.792'4—dc22

                                                   2006019550

Contents

Chapter 3: Will Nuclear Energy Be a Viable Energy Source for the Future?

Foreword

The wind farm at Altamont Pass in Northern California epitomizes many people's idea of wind power: Hundreds of towering white turbines generate electricity to power homes, factories, and businesses. The spinning turbine blades call up visions of a brighter future in which clean, renewable energy sources replace dwindling and polluting fossil fuels. The blades also kill over a thousand birds of prey each year. Every energy source, it seems, has its price.

The bird deaths at Altamont Pass make clear an unfortunate fact about all energy sources, including renewables: They have downsides. People want clean, abundant energy to power their modern lifestyles, but few want to pay the costs associated with energy production and use. Oil, coal, and natural gas contain high amounts of energy, but using them produces pollution. Commercial solar energy facilities require hundreds of acres of land and thus must be located in rural areas. Expensive and ugly transmission lines must then be run from the solar plants to the cities that need power. Producing hydrogen for fuel involves the use of dirty fossil fuels, tapping geothermal energy depletes ground water, and growing biomass for fuel ties up land that could be used to grow food. Hydroelectric power has become increasingly unpopular because dams flood vital habitats and kill wildlife and plants. Perhaps most controversial, nuclear power plants produce highly dangerous radioactive waste. People's reluctance to pay these environmental costs can be seen in the results of a 2006 Center for Economic and Civic Opinion poll. When asked how much they would support a power plant in their neighborhood, 66 percent of respondents said they would oppose it.

Many scientists warn that fossil fuel use creates emissions that threaten human health and cause global warming. Moreover, numerous scientists claim that fossil fuels are running out. As a result of these concerns, many nations have begun to revisit the energy sources that first powered human enterprises. In his 2006 State of the Union speech, U.S. President George W. Bush announced that since 2001 the United States has spent "$10 billion to develop cleaner, cheaper, and more reliable alternative energy sources," such as biomass and wind power. Despite Bush's positive rhetoric, many critics contend that the renewable energy sources he refers to are still as inefficient as they ever were and cannot possibly power modern economies. As Jerry Taylor and Peter Van Doren of the Cato Institute note, "The market share for non-hydro renewable energy . . . has languished between 1 and 3 percent for decades." Controversies such as this have been a constant throughout the history of humanity's search for the perfect energy source.

Greenhaven Press's Fueling the Future series explores this history. Each volume in the series traces the development of one energy source, and investigates the controversies surrounding its environmental impact and its potential to power humanity's future. The anthologies provide a variety of selections written by scientists, environmental activists, industry leaders, and government experts. Volumes also contain useful research tools, including an introductory essay providing important context, and an annotated table of contents that enables students to locate selections of interest easily. In addition, each volume includes an index, chronology, bibliography, glossary, and a Facts About section, which lists useful information about each energy source. Other features include numerous charts, graphs, and cartoons, which offer additional avenues for learning important information about the topic.

Fueling the Future volumes provide students with important resources for learning about the energy sources upon which human societies depend. Although it is easy to take energy for granted in developed nations, this series emphasizes how energy sources are also problematic. The U.S. Energy Information Administration calls energy "essential to life." Whether scientists will be able to develop the energy sources necessary to sustain modern life is the vital question explored in Greenhaven Press's Fueling the Future series.

Introduction

"Never has a discovery proved itself so rapidly and completely in the fulfillment of its early promises: the weapon, the submarine engine, and the power station. Never has a discovery been so technically, politically, and psychologically complex; never has the resulting technological progress suffered so many discontinuities; and never has a discovery had so many international implications and consequences."

— Bertrand Goldschmidt

I n an instant on August 6, 1945, the world was changed forever. An atomic bomb nicknamed "Little Boy" was dropped from an American B-29 bomber named *Enola Gay* on the Japanese city of Hiroshima. Over seventy thousand people were killed that day in the city. A second bomb killed another thirty-five thousand two days later in Nagasaki.

These bombings marked the arrival of the Atomic Age, which has been characterized by intense fears about atomic energy. The awesome destructive force of the atomic bomb had been clearly demonstrated in 1945, of course, and it was natural for people to fear nuclear annhiliation after learning about what happened at Hiroshima and Nagasaki. However, scientists had learned through the making of the bombs how to control a nuclear chain reaction, making peaceful applications of nuclear power, such as electricity generation, possible. Unfortunately, using nuclear power to generate electricity also provoked fears, especially following nuclear plant accidents in 1979 and 1986. In addition, people began to worry about the buildup of radioactive waste from nuclear power plants. It seems that people's fears about being harmed or killed by radiation were not confined to worries about atomic bombs.

Atoms for Peace

Of course, when peaceful uses for atomic energy were first proposed, these concerns had not yet developed. Many people believed that atomic energy offered the world a clean, new power source—one that could provide virtually limitless, affordable energy. During the 1950s President Dwight D. Eisenhower

The atomic bomb that the United States dropped on Nagasaki in 1945 ushered in the nuclear age, leaving behind a massive mushroom cloud and a devastated city.

made "Atoms for Peace" his mantra. In his famous address to the General Assembly of the United Nations, he called for the nations of the world to forego military applications of nuclear energy and instead seek peacetime uses for it.

Eisenhower was not alone in his enthusiasm. In 1955 Lewis L. Strauss, chairman of the Atomic Energy Commission predicted, "It is not too much to expect that our children will enjoy in their homes electrical energy too cheap to meter." Albert Einstein was also optimistic: "If you succeed in using the nuclear-physical findings for peaceful purposes, it will open the way to a new paradise." Scientists did find a way to use what they had learned from building atomic bombs to generate electricity with nuclear power. On December 2, 1957, the nuclear power plant at Shippingport, Pennsylvania, began the first commercial production of electricity from nuclear power.

Doubts About the Safety of Nuclear Power Emerge

The earthly paradise Einstein spoke of was not to be, however. By the 1970s doubts began to surface about nuclear power. A number of relatively minor accidents at nuclear power plants prompted the production and release of the 1979 movie *The China Syndrome*. The movie featured two reporters on a visit to a nuclear power plant. During their visit they inadvertently videotape a crisis in the plant's control room. The reactor has a near meltdown, and plant management covers up the event. People who watched the movie took away two messages: Nuclear power plants are dangerous, and the people who run them cannot be trusted. Coincidentally, twelve days after the movie was released, on March 28, 1979, a real accident at the Three Mile Island nuclear power plant in Pennsylvania resulted in a small amount of radioactive steam being released. The dramatized accident in the movie and the real accident at Three Mile Island resulted in a public galvanized against nuclear power.

Further adding to people's fears was the accident at the Chernobyl nuclear power plant on April 25, 1986, in the Soviet Union. Bad design, poor construction, lax safety standards, and operator error all contributed to the worst nuclear

A 1979 photo shows the cooling towers at the Three Mile Island nuclear plant in Pennsylvania after the facility was shut down.

disaster in history. In the words of then Soviet leader Mikhail Gorbachev, "For the first time ever, we have confronted in reality the sinister power of uncontrolled nuclear energy."

The accidents at Three Mile Island and Chernobyl essentially shut down the nuclear power industry. The last new nuclear power plants ordered in the United States were commissioned in 1978, and all of them were eventually cancelled. Fear—irrational fear, some said—put all further developments on hold as the issues surrounding nuclear power became highly politicized.

The Debate over Nuclear Power Intensifies

Proponents of nuclear power tried to minimize the significance of the Three Mile Island and Chernobyl accidents. They argued that although these were serious accidents, they were the only two of such magnitude that had occurred since the first nuclear power plant was built. These advocates pointed out that the nuclear power industry's safety record, then, was quite good, especially considering the number of nuclear power plants operating throughout the world. Nuclear supporters also dismissed concerns about nuclear waste. "All the waste in a year from a nuclear power plant can be stored under a desk," President Ronald Reagan once remarked. He was right, supporters of nuclear power contended. In fact, they claimed, if all of the nuclear waste created in the United States was placed on a football field, the pile would be only fifteen feet deep.

Detractors, however, saw the nuclear waste problem somewhat differently. Some waste is dangerous for thousands of years, they pointed out, which means that waste created today would be left for future generations to deal with. Critics questioned whether this waste could be stored safely for such long periods of time. Moreover, critics of nuclear power were not moved by supporters' positive interpretation of the Three Mile Island and Chernobyl accidents. They argued that if one or two such accidents could occur, it was extremely likely that more would occur in the future. Further, they pointed out, these accidents could be even worse.

The cost of nuclear power has also been a concern. As long as oil and gas prices remained low throughout the 1980s and 1990s, fossil fuel plants were deemed cheaper to run than nuclear power plants. The twenty-first century has brought changes, however. Rising oil and gas prices have made electricity generated from fossil fuels more expensive. Suddenly, nuclear power has become more competitive. Moreover, concern that the burning of fossil fuels is contributing to global warming has renewed interest in nuclear power, which does not produce greenhouse gas emissions. The industry that many assumed had no future now seems ready to prosper again.

The Future of Nuclear Power

As the world population continues to grow and energy needs increase, nations around the world are rethinking their energy plans. For example, while the United States has abundant supplies of coal, that fuel produces dangerous emissions when burned. Burning oil and gas also produces greenhouse gases, and many experts say that supplies of these energy sources are dwindling. Alternatives such as hydroelectric, solar, and wind power do not produce enough energy as yet to meet the needs of a growing population, according to numerous experts.

Considering the drawbacks of these energy sources, many nations are reconsidering nuclear power. U.S. president George W. Bush made nuclear power an important part of his energy policy. American utilities now are applying for permits to begin the process of expanding their nuclear power–generating capacity. Whether this renewed interest in nuclear power will continue, or whether fears about nuclear accidents and radioactive waste will once again put a stop to the construction of new nuclear power plants remains to be seen. The debate about nuclear safety will continue, but even as it does, economic necessity may inevitably increase the role of nuclear power in meeting future energy needs.

Otto Hahn (left) and Fritz Strassmann (center) won the Nobel Prize for their experiment demonstrating the splitting of uranium atoms by neutrons.

CHAPTER 1

The Development of Nuclear Power

The History of Nuclear Power

U.S. Department of Energy

This selection from the Department of Energy (DOE), which establishes the U.S. government's energy policies, traces the history of nuclear power. According to the DOE, nuclear power was first harnessed for use in atomic bombs during World War II. Nuclear bombs were dropped on the Japanese cities of Hiroshima and Nagasaki, effectively ending the war. During the 1950s peaceful applications of atomic energy were explored. By the 1970s numerous nuclear power plants had been built, supplying the United States with electricity. However, an accident at the Three Mile Island nuclear power plant in 1979 led to concerns over the safety of nuclear energy, and by the mid-1980s construction of new nuclear plants in America had ceased.

I n 1938, two German physicists, Otto Hahn and Fritz Strassman, discovered that a neutron caused the nucleus of a uranium atom to split (fission). Other experiments followed that showed that the energy released in fission was about 100 million times greater than a chemical reaction. At the onset of World War II, the military implications of this discovery were readily apparent to leaders of the major powers. Uranium was destined to find new, more important applications beyond its original use as a colorant for glass and ceramics.

U.S. Department of Energy, "Uranium Stewardship Activities," www.ne.doe.gov/uranium/history.html, February 28, 2006.

Nuclear Research Began with Military Applications

In the early 1940s, U.S. intelligence regarding Germany's promising nuclear research activities dramatically hastened the United States's resolve to build a nuclear weapon. The Manhattan Project was established for this purpose in August 1942. At the University of Chicago in December 1942, Enrico Fermi and his team created a controlled, self-sustaining chain reaction using uranium and a crude graphite-pile reactor. This discovery accelerated nuclear research being conducted in the U.S.

One of the leaders of the Manhattan Project, Enrico Fermi demonstrates complex physics equations at the University of Chicago in 1954.

In July 1945, Manhattan Project scientists tested the first nuclear device in Alamagordo, New Mexico, using plutonium produced from a uranium and graphite-pile reactor in Richland, Washington. A month later a highly enriched uranium nuclear bomb was dropped on the Japanese city of Hiroshima, and a plutonium nuclear bomb was dropped on Nagasaki, effectively ending World War II.

As the primary raw ingredient for the first generation of atomic weapons, uranium had quickly evolved to become a resource of vital importance to U.S. national security as well as to the security of the fragile, post-war Western alliance.

Exploring Peaceful Uses of Atomic Energy

At the time, only the Federal Government could produce and use enriched uranium in the United States. In August 1946, President [Harry] Truman signed the Atomic Energy Act that established the Atomic Energy Commission as the Federal entity responsible for developing and producing nuclear weapons as well as for research on other uses for nuclear energy. President [Dwight] Eisenhower initiated the Atoms for Peace Program in 1953 to promote peaceful uses and commercial applications of nuclear power. In 1954, Congress approved amendments to the Atomic Energy Act that provided direction and support for development of commercial nuclear power. . . .

Commercial Use of Nuclear Energy

The 1950s were a decade of spectacular achievement in nuclear energy: only two decades after the initial experiments with nuclear energy sources, both peaceful and defense applications were well underway. The first nuclear-powered submarine, the USS *Nautilus*, was launched in 1954, and in 1955, Arco, Idaho, became the first U.S. town to be powered by nuclear energy

The USS Nautilus, the world's first nuclear-powered submarine, is shown in an aerial view in 1959.

using electricity produced at the Idaho National Energy Laboratory.

The rise of commercial nuclear power plants greatly expanded the demand for uranium. Building of the world's first large-scale nuclear power plant began in Shippingport, Pennsylvania, in 1954, signaling the start of a rapidly developed first generation of commercial nuclear power plants. By 1957, this plant was operating and producing electricity in the Pittsburgh area. In 1959, the first privately funded nuclear power plant, Dresden Nuclear Power Station, began operating in Morris, Illinois.

To meet the increasing demand for enriched uranium, the Department of Energy (DOE) built two gaseous diffusion plants. These plants began operating in 1954 and 1956, respectively, and supplemented the Government's already existing uranium enrichment operation.

Nuclear Power Goes Private

Throughout this period, the Federal Government continued to provide all uranium enrichment services. In 1964, a major change

In 1957 in Shippingport, Pennsylvania, scientists and workers place the reactor core into position at the first nuclear power plant.

came about with passage of the Private Ownership of Special Nuclear Materials Act (Public Law 88-489) that amended the Atomic Energy Act of 1954 (Public Law 88-489). This amendment made it possible for utilities to purchase and own enriched uranium for use in commercial nuclear power plants. The burgeoning demand for uranium greatly contributed to the growth of the U.S. uranium mining industry. By the end of the 1970s, 70 commercial nuclear power plants were operating in the United States.

However, a slowdown started in the mid-1970s due to a slower than projected increase in the demand for electricity and more stringent regulations that greatly increased the time and cost of constructing and licensing new plants. The accident in 1979 of Unit #2 of the Three Mile Island nuclear power plant near Harrisburg, Pennsylvania, contributed to the downturn, and by the 1980s, the whole U.S. nuclear industry was faltering. In 1984 alone, 16 nuclear power plant projects in the United States were canceled.

Nuclear Power Should Be Used for Peaceful Purposes

Dwight D. Eisenhower

The following selection is excerpted from a speech that has become known as the "Atoms for Peace" address. President Dwight D. Eisenhower delivered this speech to the General Assembly of the United Nations on December 8, 1953. In it he outlines his plan for controlling nuclear weapons while developing peaceful uses for atomic energy. As Eisenhower explains, since the United States used nuclear bombs during World War II, many other countries began developing them. This proliferation of dangerous weapons has raised the specter of nuclear annihilation, he notes. Therefore, Eisenhower concludes, nations need to begin using nuclear energy for peaceful purposes—such as electricity generation—rather than for bombs. The president's speech ushered in an age of peaceful use of atomic energy to power homes, businesses, and factories.

I feel impelled to speak today in a language that in a sense is new—one which I, who have spent so much of my life in the military profession, would have preferred never to use.

That new language is the language of atomic warfare.

The Dangers of Atomic Weapons

The atomic age has moved forward at such a pace that every citizen of the world should have some comprehension, at least

President Dwight D. Eisenhower, Speech Before the General Assembly of the UN on Peaceful Uses of Atomic Energy, New York City, December 8, 1953.

Addressing the United Nations in 1953, President Dwight D. Eisenhower asks for peaceful nuclear applications in his "Atoms for Peace" speech.

in comparative terms, of the extent of this development of the utmost significance to every one of us. Clearly, if the people of the world are to conduct an intelligent search for peace, they must be armed with the significant facts of today's existence.

My recital of atomic danger and power is necessarily stated in United States terms, for these are the only incontrovertible facts that I know. I need hardly point out to this [United Nations General] Assembly, however, that this subject is global, not merely national in character.

On July 16, 1945, the United States set off the world's first atomic explosion. Since that date in 1945, the United States of America has conducted 42 test explosions.

Atomic bombs today are more than 25 times as powerful as the weapons with which the atomic age dawned, while hydrogen weapons are in the ranges of millions of tons of TNT equivalent.

Today, the United States' stockpile of atomic weapons, which, of course, increases daily, exceeds by many times the explosive equivalent of the total of all bombs and all shells that came from every plane and every gun in every theatre of war in all of the years of World War II. A single air group, whether afloat or land-based, can now deliver to any reachable target a destructive cargo exceeding in power all the bombs that fell on Britain in all of World War II.

In size and variety, the development of atomic weapons has been no less remarkable. The development has been such that atomic weapons have virtually achieved conventional status within our armed services. In the United States, the Army, the Navy, the Air Force, and the Marine Corps are all capable of putting this weapon to military use.

Nuclear Weapons Have Spread Across the Globe

But the dread secret, and the fearful engines of atomic might, are not ours alone. In the first place, the secret is possessed by our friends and allies, Great Britain and Canada, whose scientific genius made a tremendous contribution to our original discoveries, and the designs of atomic bombs.

The secret is also known by the Soviet Union. The Soviet Union has informed us that, over recent years, it has devoted extensive resources to atomic weapons. During this period, the Soviet Union has exploded a series of atomic devices, including at least one involving thermo-nuclear reactions.

If at one time the United States possessed what might have been called a monopoly of atomic power, that monopoly ceased to exist several years ago. Therefore, although our earlier start has permitted us to accumulate what is today a great quantitative advantage, the atomic realities of today comprehend two facts of even greater significance.

First, the knowledge now possessed by several nations will eventually be shared by others—possibly all others. Second, even a vast superiority in numbers of weapons, and a consequent capability of devastating retaliation, is no preventive, of itself, against the fearful material damage and toll of human lives that would be inflicted by surprise aggression.

The free world, at least dimly aware of these facts, has naturally embarked on a large program of warning and defense systems. That program will be accelerated and expanded. But let no one think that the expenditure of vast sums for weapons and

During a parade in Moscow's Red Square in 1963, the Soviet Union displays the might of its nuclear rocket arsenal.

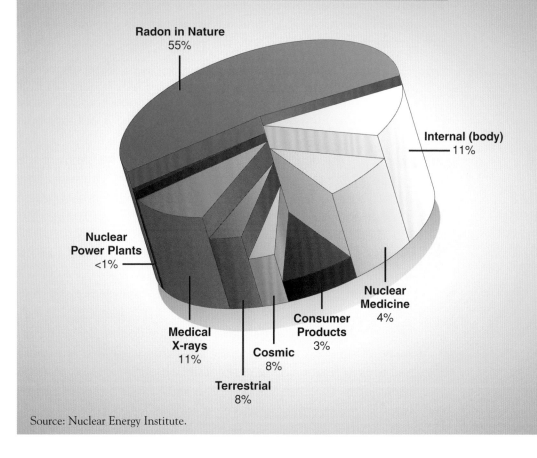

Public Exposure to Radiation

Radon in Nature
55%

Internal (body)
11%

Nuclear Power Plants
<1%

Nuclear Medicine
4%

Consumer Products
3%

Medical X-rays
11%

Cosmic
8%

Terrestrial
8%

Source: Nuclear Energy Institute.

systems of defense can guarantee absolute safety for the cities and citizens of any nation. The awful arithmetic of the atomic bomb does not permit any such easy solution. Even against the most powerful defense, an aggressor in possession of the effective minimum number of atomic bombs for a surprise attack could probably place a sufficient number of his bombs on the chosen targets to cause hideous damage. . . .

The United States Wants to End the Arms Race

The United States, heeding the suggestion of the General Assembly of the United Nations, is instantly prepared to meet privately with such other countries as may be "principally involved," to seek "an acceptable solution" to the atomic armaments race which overshadows not only the peace, but the very life, of the world.

We shall carry into these private or diplomatic talks a new conception. The United States would seek more than the mere reduction or elimination of atomic materials for military purposes.

It is not enough to take this weapon out of the hands of the soldiers. It must be put into the hands of those who will know how to strip its military casing and adapt it to the arts of peace. The United States knows that if the fearful trend of atomic military build up can be reversed, this greatest of destructive forces can be developed into a great boon, for the benefit of all mankind.

The United States knows that peaceful power from atomic energy is no dream of the future. That capability, already proved, is here—now—today. Who can doubt, if the entire body of the world's scientists and engineers had adequate amounts of fissionable material with which to test and develop their ideas, that this capability would rapidly be transformed into universal, efficient, and economic usage.

To hasten the day when fear of the atom will begin to disappear from the minds of people, and the governments of the East and West, there are certain steps that can be taken now.

The Creation of the Atomic Energy Agency

I therefore make the following proposals:

The Governments principally involved, to the extent permitted by elementary prudence, to begin now and continue to make joint contributions from their stockpiles of normal uranium and fissionable materials to an international Atomic Energy Agency. We would expect that such an agency would be set up under the aegis of the United Nations. . . .

The United states is prepared to undertake these explorations in good faith. Any partner of the United States acting in the same good faith will find the United States a not unreasonable or ungenerous associate.

Undoubtedly initial and early contributions to this plan would be small in quantity. However, the proposal has the great virtue that it can be undertaken without the irritations and mutual suspicions incident to any attempt to set up a completely acceptable system of world-wide inspection and control.

The Atomic Energy Agency could be made responsible for the impounding, storage, and protection of the contributed fissionable and other materials. The ingenuity of our scientists will provide special safe conditions under which such a bank of fissionable material can be made essentially immune to surprise seizure.

This nuclear plant under construction in 1955 illustrates the peaceful application of atomic power that President Eisenhower raised.

The more important responsibility of this Atomic Energy Agency would be to devise methods where by this fissionable material would be allocated to serve the peaceful pursuits of mankind. Experts would be mobilized to apply atomic energy to the needs of agriculture, medicine, and other peaceful activities. A special purpose would be to provide abundant electrical energy in the power-starved areas of the world. Thus the contributing powers would be dedicating some of their strength to serve the needs rather than the fears of mankind.

The United States would be more than willing—it would be proud—to take up with others "principally involved" the development of plans where by such peaceful use of atomic energy would be expedited.

Of those "principally involved" the Soviet Union must, of course, be one.

Initiating a New Vision for Atomic Power

I would be prepared to submit to the Congress of the United States, and with every expectation of approval, any such plan that would:

First—encourage world-wide investigation into the most effective peacetime uses of fissionable material, and with the certainty that they had all the material needed for the conduct of all experiments that were appropriate;

Second—begin to diminish the potential destructive power of the world's atomic stockpiles;

Third—allow all peoples of all nations to see that, in this enlightened age, the great powers of the earth, both of the East and of the West, are interested in human aspirations first, rather than in building up the armaments of war;

Fourth—open up a new channel for peaceful discussion, and initiate at least a new approach to the many difficult problems that must be solved in both private and public conversations, if the world is to shake off the inertia imposed by fear, and is to make positive progress toward peace.

Against the dark background of the atomic bomb, the United States does not wish merely to present strength, but also the desire and the hope for peace.

The Three Mile Island Accident Derails Nuclear Power

Joel Helgerson

> In this selection author Joel Helgerson describes the acci-
> dent at the Three Mile Island nuclear power plant, which
> brought the construction of new nuclear power plants to
> a halt. He explains how a combination of operator error
> and equipment failure contributed to the 1979 accident at
> the Harrisburg, Pennsylvania, plant. Increased fear about
> nuclear power combined with more stringent safety regu-
> lations effectively put a stop to the construction of new
> plants in the United States.

Early in the morning on March 28, 1978, a maintenance crew was cleaning the polishers in the secondary cooling loop of reactor number 2 [of the Three Mile Island nuclear plant]. On this day, reactor 1 was shut down for refueling, but reactor 2, where the accident occurred, was running at 97 per-cent of its capacity.

The Crisis Began with Routine Maintenance

At thirty-six seconds past 4:00 A.M., the movement of water through the secondary cooling system stopped because of a block-age in the system's polishers. The maintenance crew had been removing resin-coated pellets from the polishers. The pellets

Joel Helgerson, from *Nuclear Accidents*. Franklin Watts, 1988. Copyright © 1988 by Joel Helgerson. All rights reserved. Reprinted by permission of Franklin Watts, an imprint of Scholastic Library Publishing, Inc.

absorbed unwanted minerals from the water. Cleaning them was a normal maintenance procedure that was done about once a month.

While the resin-coated pellets were being transferred out of the secondary cooling loop, the flow of water through the loop became blocked. This started a chain reaction that within seconds shut off the steam turbine and brought the flow of liquid in the secondary cooling loop to a complete halt. The primary result of this shutdown was that the secondary loop stopped absorbing heat from the primary cooling system. This caused the core temperature to quickly rise.

The plant operators in the control room did not at first realize that the secondary cooling loop was blocked. But after a few seconds had passed, the steam turbine "tripped" (shut off), and a light and a beeper (called an *annunciator*) warned them of the problem.

Emergency Procedures Begin

Two things should now have automatically happened in response to the problem. First, control rods should have fallen into the core of the reactor. This [emergency] procedure is meant to reduce the speed of the fission process in the core and thus the amount of heat produced. The [procedure] happened as it was supposed to, and within nine seconds, sixty-nine control rods fell into place. At the same time, the pressurizer's relief valve opened so that some of the pressure in the primary cooling loop could be released. When the pressure reached a safe level, the pressurizer's relief valve was supposed to automatically close. It didn't. The valve stuck open and steam continued to rush out the valve at a rate of 110,000 pounds (50,000 kg) per hour. This was approximately equal to losing 220 gallons (830 liters) of water a minute.

The second thing that was supposed to happen was that auxiliary feedwater pumps should have started pumping water to the secondary system. The auxiliary pumps started up as they were supposed to, but the operators failed to notice that the valves on the pipes leading to the auxiliary pumps were closed. (One indicator was obscured by a hanging caution tag; the other may have been obscured by an operator's body as he leaned over the panel.)

The accident at Three Mile Island that damaged reactor number 2 in 1979 occurred in the blue building between the two cooling towers in the foreground.

This meant that they were unable to add water to the secondary system. Eight minutes passed before the operators noticed that the light indicators for these valves showed they were closed. At that time the valves were manually opened.

Operators Struggled to Contain the Damage

The plant operators were now playing a major role in the development of the accident. The operators had been instructed that the primary means for determining whether or not the reactor core was losing coolant was the water-level indicator in the pressurizer. As long as this showed a high level of water the operators were trained to believe that there was sufficient water in the

This picture shows the broken fuel assemblies adhering to the bottom of the Three Mile Island's damaged reactor unit 2.

primary cooling loop. The flaw in their training and with the written emergency procedures they were using was that no one had ever envisioned that the relief valve at the top of the pressurizer might accidentally remain stuck in the open position.

As the pressure level in the primary cooling loop dropped, the emergency core-cooling system automatically turned on, and the high-pressure injection pumps pushed water into the primary loop. At this point the operators made a serious error in judgment. Seeing by the gauges that the pressurizer contained a high level of water, they believed that too much water was being added to the primary cooling loop. One thing their training had emphasized was that they shouldn't allow the pressurizer to fill completely with water. If that happened, they would lose the ability to regulate pressure in the system. To avoid this, they manually overrode the emergency core-cooling system and reduced the flow of water from the high-pressure injection pumps. What they didn't realize was that the water-level indicator in the pressurizer wasn't high because there was too much water in the system. It was high because water was flowing through the pressurizer and out the relief valve that was stuck open, into a coolant drain tank. The system was losing water fast. A loss-of-coolant accident was happening, but the operators believed just the opposite.

Two hours and eighteen minutes passed before the plant operators realized the relief valve was stuck open. Not until that

On April 2, 1979, members of the Nuclear Regulatory Commission give a press conference addressing the nuclear accident at Three Mile Island.

time did they close it. Engineers would later speculate that if the relief valve had been left open another half hour to an hour, the core of the reactor might have been without coolant and could have completely melted down.

The Crisis Worsens

Under normal conditions, the core of the reactor was covered by 6 feet (1.8 m) of water, but with the relief valve stuck open, this water slowly drained away. The temperature in the core rose faster, eventually topping 2,000° F (1,100° C). Some parts of the reactor heated up to 5,000° F (2,750° C), and the uranium fuel pellets began to melt.

At the same time, a chemical reaction was taking place between the water turning to steam and the zirconium alloy of the fuel rods. The zirconium took the oxygen from the steam molecules and formed zirconium oxide. This process freed hydrogen from the steam molecules. Hydrogen gas is highly explosive.

During all of this, the operators believed the core was covered with water. The system pressure continued to be low, but the water level indicators for the pressurizer stayed high—a contradiction the operators were unable to explain. . . .

Core Meltdown Was Averted

By 4:00 P.M., twelve hours after the accident started, plant personnel had correctly diagnosed the problem and used the high-pressure injection pumps to force additional water into the core and cool it. The danger of a core meltdown was now past. . . .

The Three Mile Island accident has also affected the regulation of safety at other nuclear power plants in the United States. In particular, the accident resulted in more stringent requirements for emergency plans in the event of an accident. . . .

One outgrowth of the . . . regulations is that they have allowed state and local governments to prevent the licensing of new nuclear power plants. This happened because the local governments must now approve of a plant's evacuation plans before the NRC [Nuclear Regulatory Commission] can grant the plant an operating license. Such control of plants by states has effectively blocked the start-up of any new nuclear power plants in the United States.

The Chernobyl disaster was caused by sub-standard safety regulations and outdated technology.

CHAPTER 2

Is Nuclear Power Safe?

The Threat of a Major Nuclear Power Plant Accident Is Serious

Peter Bunyard

In this selection Peter Bunyard catalogs a history of accidents in the United States and Europe. While the nuclear industry claims to take extraordinary measures to safeguard plant facilities, Bunyard claims, nuclear power plants are not really safe. The numerous serious accidents, notably at Three Mile Island in the United States and at Chernobyl in the Ukraine, illustrate that nuclear power is inherently dangerous. Bunyard is an author and a founding editor of *Ecologist*, a magazine about environmental affairs.

Nuclear power is safer than ever. The chance of an accident happening at a nuclear plant is virtually nil. Windscale and Three Mile Island were a long time ago, and Chernobyl was a result of lax safety standards and primitive technology.[1] Modern nuclear technology is virtually infallible. Or so the industry tells us. . . .

When we survey the history of the nuclear industry in any part of the world, we see a catalogue of accidents, disasters and near-misses. We see an inherently unsafe technology which, from its inception in the 1940s has been plagued by accidents small and large; some of which came to light, others which were covered up. We see that it is by luck rather than judgement that the Western world has not suffered the equivalent of Chernobyl or worse.

Peter Bunyard, "It Couldn't happen Here," Ecologist, Vol. 29, November, 1999, p. 402.
Copyright © 1999 MIT Press Journals. Reproduced by Permission.

Nuclear Accidents Have Been Hidden

The problems suffered by the nuclear industry surfaced almost as soon as the first reactor became operational and they have continued to plague us. The first ever experimental fast reactor, EBR-1, sited at the US government base at Idaho, began operating in December 1951. Just four years later, it very nearly blew its top because of a runaway chain reaction caused by the fuel creeping and distorting inside the core. The reactor was no more than half a second away from exploding, when a scientist bystander had the presence of mind to press the button that allowed the reactor core to drop away, so bringing the chain reaction to an end. Few people know about this; had another half a second elapsed, the whole world would have done. But it is not an exception; it is typical of nuclear power's safety record right from its earliest years.

The Fermi fast reactor, less than 20 miles outside Detroit, began life in 1963. It suffered innumerable teething problems, including creeping of fuel elements under intense neuron bombardment, sodium corrosion of metallic structures in the core and subsequent problems with the steam-generating plant. Three years later, as the operators were taking the reactor up to full power, a loose metal flange jammed across some fuel elements and prevented the flow of liquid sodium coolant. The heating caused some fuel elements to bow in towards each other and the power took off. Luckily the accident was limited to just one part of the core, and luckily too the operators managed to prevent a major explosion. If not, Detroit would have been lost.

More Nuclear Accidents

The notorious fire at the Windscale No. 1 plutonium pile in October 1958, was, at the time, the worst accident to hit the nuclear industry in the West. It resulted from the building-up of pent-up energy, because of the constant bombardment by neutrons. This energy was routinely released by raising the power of

---

1. The power plants mentioned all suffered accidents that resulted in the release of radioactive substances into the nearby areas.

The Windscale atomic reactor in Yorkshire, England (shown here in 1960), sustained damage from a fire in 1958.

the reactor so as to heat up the graphite moderator and then letting the core cool down. But it went wrong, and the graphite overheated to the point where it caught fire, even though bathed with hot carbon dioxide gas. The intense heat caused uranium fuel to catch fire and the two started burning furiously together. Fortunately (though almost as an afterthought) the designers had added a filter to the reactor chimney; without this, the release of volatile fission products such as iodine, caesium and strontium as well as small particles of plutonium would have been far worse. As it was, as much as 20,000 curies of iodine-131 escaped into the atmosphere, which with the remaining radionuclides may have resulted in up to 1,000 premature deaths, according to the UK [United Kingdom] National Radiological Protection Board.

Nuclear accidents do not only occur within the reactors themselves. A year before the Windscale accident, the Soviet Union had experienced an explosion in a nuclear waste repository at Kyshtym, which devastated more than 13,000 square kilometres and—like Chernobyl would later do—led to villages being evacuated. It is not known how many deaths resulted from this. Just before the Windscale Inquiry in 1977, scientist Zhores Medvedev, who had carried out radioecological studies on flora and fauna in the Kyshtym area before defecting to the UK, pointed to Kyshtym as exemplifying some of the risks associated with nuclear waste management. The then-head of the UK Atomic Energy Authority, Sir John Hill, publicly derided Medvedev, announcing that the Kyshtym disaster was "rubbish—a figment of the imagination . . . pure science fiction." But radio-isotope analysis later carried out at the US government's Oak Ridge Laboratory, showed that the accident had probably resulted from the failure of a cooling system in a nuclear waste repository.

In addition to reactor explosions and problems with waste dumps, accidental radioactive releases into the atmosphere have been a regular feature of the nuclear age. Indeed, British Nuclear Fuels, through their reprocessing and nuclear waste activities, have released sufficient radioactive waste into the environment to be on a par with all but the worst accidents. Over a 15-year period, from 1961 to 1977, discharges of caesium-137 went up more than 100-fold to 120,000 curies a year. According to its own admission at the 1977 Windscale Inquiry, between 1950 and 1977 Windscale had suffered 194 reportable incidents, 11 of which involved fires or explosions and 45 of which involved releases of plutonium into the environment. A German study of reactor safety in 1980 showed that during 1976 and 1977 commercial power plants had suffered accidents on average once every three days. In 1976, out of 139 accidents in all, 24 involved the release of "more than permissible amounts of radioactivity."

The Chernobyl Accident

At Chernobyl, in 1986, is the most notorious nuclear accident the world has yet known. The operators were carrying out a test in which they hoped to show that sufficient power could be obtained from the turbines during a sudden shut-down to ensure that essential safety systems would run before back-up diesels kicked in. In other words, it was a safety test that caused the accident. In essence, the explosion at Chernobyl was caused because the operators tried simultaneously to keep the power down and the temperature up, which they did by disengaging the automatic "scram" (safety) system, and by trying to regulate water pressure in the reactor. They got it wrong, and within a few seconds the power soared uncontrollably and they had a slow, but fatal, atomic bomb on their hands.

It Couldn't Happen Here

Ever since Chernobyl, the public in the West has repeatedly been assured that "it couldn't happen here." The nuclear industry has tried hard to distance itself from the Soviet RBMK reactor design (of which the Chernobyl reactor was an example), as if it were flawed in ways that would never be tolerated in the West. In fact, though—and crucially—this is not the case. The RBMK reactor is not very different in concept and design from reactors currently operating across Europe and the USA.

In the UK we have six AGR (advanced gas reactor) stations, each with twin reactors. Like Chernobyl, the AGR uses a graphite moderator, but carbon dioxide instead of water as coolant. The fuel is encased in stainless steel tubes. John Large, adviser to both government and Greenpeace on nuclear safety matters, baldly stated after Chernobyl that AGRs were essentially "benign" reactors, and supposedly immune from a Chernobyl-like explosion.

Yet, as Philip Cade and I demonstrated in a 1987 report for Greenpeace, entitled *Chernobyl UK*, AGRs have the potential for accidents just as catastrophic as that of Chernobyl. For example, a sequence of events in which the AGR's gas circulatory system failed, followed by a failure of the reactor to shut down could lead within minutes to a massive explosion, far in excess of that which destroyed Chernobyl. The key to that event would be the melting of the steel cladding from the fuel at a faster rate than the fuel would collapse. Steel is a potent absorber of neutrons and its "sloughing off" would free enough "prompt" neutrons to push up the chain reaction to the critical point.

Having created a mathematical model of the AGR, in which he could follow the course of a potential accident, nuclear engineer Richard Webb gave a critical review of our Greenpeace thesis. Whereas the UK Atomic Energy Authority and the Electricity Board had denied that an accident involving gas circulatory failure and failure to shut-down would lead to an explosion, on the grounds that the fuel would first melt into a non-critical state (a nonetheless major admission), Webb showed that the accident

This photo shows all that remained of reactor number 4 after the deadly nuclear catastrophe at Chernobyl in 1986.

In this undated photo, construction is underway on a sarcophagus to seal in the radioactive materials inside reactor number 4 at Chernobyl.

could be far worse than envisaged, because vaporising fuel would increase substantially the rate of neutron production and lead to an escalation in the runaway chain reaction. In effect, the reactor's power would increase thousands of times above maximum operating power in a matter of seconds.

A Nuclear Catastrophe Could Happen Again

As our Greenpeace report pointed out, one of the criticisms of the Russian-built RBMK reactor was its poor containment by Western standards. Yet, in one of those paradoxical twists, that "failing" allowed the reactor to explode early on and therefore with less impact than were the containment to have held longer. Just imagine if the explosion had been big enough to destroy the other two working reactors then in operation at Chernobyl—the result would have been a virtual holocaust.

AGRs are certainly designed to contain any accidents more effectively than are Soviet reactors. They have a massive 7-metre thick reinforced concrete pressure vessel which, in order for it to be blown apart, a combination of events, in which both the coolant circulators and the scramming of control rods fail simultaneously, would be necessary. While this is highly improbable, the gas circulators in AGRs have failed on several occasions—one being during the storm that caused power to fail at Hinkley Point in Somerset in the winter of 1990.

Just after the Chernobyl accident, when the nuclear industry was congratulating itself that such a disaster would be most unlikely in the West, the US Nuclear Regulatory Commissioner, James Asselstine, remarked with regard to commercial reactors in the US: "The bottom line is that, given the present level of safety being achieved by the operating nuclear power plants in this country, we can expect to see a core meltdown accident within the next 20 years; and it is possible that such an accident could result in off-site releases of radiation which are as large as, or larger than, the releases estimated to have occurred at Chernobyl."

The real bottom line is that nuclear power, wherever it is in the world, whatever safety standards imposed and whatever reassurances its advocates give, is an inherently unsafe technology. Its history so far amply demonstrates this simple fact. The only truly safe option is to shut it down permanently.

Nuclear Power Plants Have Become Safer

Nuclear Energy Institute

This selection is excerpted from a handbook prepared by the Nuclear Energy Institute, an industry trade association. The NEI contends that nuclear power has gotten safer since the Three Mile Island power plant accident in 1979. Engineers learned from that event, NEI maintains, and now build multiple safety features into the nuclear power generation process. Moreover, after the accident two oversight agencies were created to make sure that nuclear power plants are run safely.

A nuclear power plant is a way to boil water to generate steam without the use of fossil fuels. The steam turns a turbine to produce electricity, just as it does in any power plant. The difference is that in a nuclear plant, the heat used to generate steam is produced by a nuclear reaction involving uranium, instead of by the combustion of fossil fuel. The reactor's uranium is manufactured in solid pellets, each about a half-inch long. The pellets are stacked by the hundreds into long, thin fuel rods bundled to form fuel assemblies, with the number of assemblies in the typical reactor ranging from 550 to 800. All the fuel assemblies together are referred to as the reactor "core."

Two Types of Reactors

In the United States, there are two main types of light water reactors: the pressurized water reactor (PWR) and the boiling

Nuclear Energy Institute "Section 1. Plant Safety," Guide to Nuclear Energy, January 2001, pp. 5–10. Reproduced by permission.

water reactor (BWR). Pressurized water reactors outnumber boiling water reactors by 2-1. Both types operate on basically the same principles, and both are cooled using ordinary water.

In a PWR, heated water passing through the core is kept under high pressure so that it will not boil. The water is piped to a steam generator, a kind of heat exchanger, and the steam thus formed drives the turbine. After the steam passes through

Boiling Water Reactor (BWR)

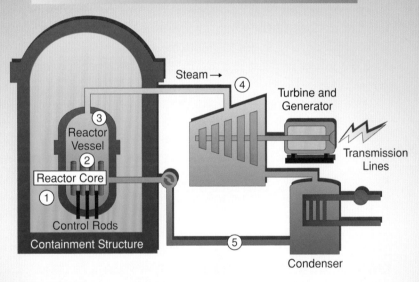

In a typical boiling water reactor:
1. The reactor core creates heat.
2. A steam-water mixture is produced when very pure water (reactor coolant) moves upward through the core absorbing heat.
3. The steam-water mixture leaves the top of the core and enters the two stages of moisture separation where water droplets are removed before the steam is allowed to enter the steam line.
4. The steam line directs the steam to the main turbine causing it to turn the turbine generator, which produces electricity.
5. The unused steam is exhausted to the condenser where it is condensed into water. The resulting water is pumped out of the condenser with a series of pumps, reheated, and pumped back to the reactor vessel.

Source: www.euronuclear.org

the turbine, it then passes through a heat exchanger called a condenser. Water circulates through tubes in the condenser, cooling the used steam and converting it to water again. The condensed water is then returned to the steam generator and the cycle is repeated.

In a BWR, heated water passing through the core is allowed to boil after it leaves the core. The boiling water produces steam that drives the turbine. After the steam passes through the turbine and the condenser, it is reused in the reactor.

Multiple Safety Systems Are in Place

A nuclear plant in the United States has multiple backup safety systems to provide "defense in depth." Safety features are built in to control the chain reaction. Control rods absorb tiny subatomic particles called neutrons and control the reaction. The reactor core itself is contained within a steel pressure vessel with very thick walls.

Water helps moderate the reaction inside the reactor. Although the control rods are the main way to control the nuclear reaction, the water helps, too. The greater the nuclear reaction, the more heat is produced. The increasing heat turns more water to steam, which slows down the nuclear reaction. So the water works like a brake. It prevents the nuclear reaction from running out of control. If the water were ever lost, multiple emergency cooling systems would keep the reactor from overheating.

The "defense in depth" philosophy recognizes that equipment can fail and that operators can make mistakes. So the plant has built-in sensors to watch temperature, pressure, water level and other indicators that are important to safety. These sensors are linked to control systems that adjust or shut down the plant—immediately and automatically—at the first sign of trouble. These safety mechanisms operate independently, and each has one or more backups: If one set fails, another is available for safe shutdown of the reactor.

U.S. nuclear power plants also use a series of physical barriers to make sure that radioactive material does not escape. The first barrier is the composition of nuclear fuel itself. The radioactive byproducts of the fission process remain locked inside the fuel pellets. These pellets are sealed inside rods made of special metal. The fuel rods are positioned inside a large steel vessel, which has walls about eight inches thick. At most plants, the reactor and vessel are enclosed in a large, leak-tight shell of steel

Pressurized Water Reactor (PWR)

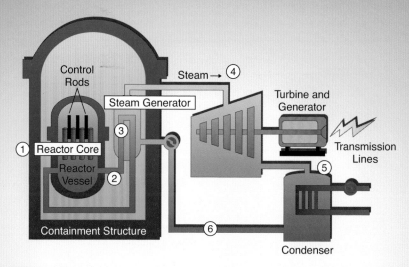

PWRs keep water under pressure so that it heats up but does not boil. Water from the reactor and water in the steam generator never mix.

In a typical commercial pressurized water reactor:
1. The reactor core generates heat.
2. Pressurized-water in the primary coolant loop carries the heat to the steam generator.
3. Inside the steam generator, heat from the primary coolant loop vaporizes the water in a secondary loop, producing steam.
4. The steam line directs the steam to the main turbine causing it to turn the turbine generator, which produces electricity.
5. The unused steam is exhausted to the condenser where it is condensed into water.
6. The resulting water is pumped out of the condenser with a series of pumps, reheated, and pumped back to the steam generator.

Source: www.euronuclear.org

plate. All this is contained inside a massive, reinforced-concrete structure—called the containment—with walls that are typically three to four feet thick.

The many thick layers of the containment building keep radioactive materials safely inside. Without question, the 1986 accident at Chernobyl in the former Soviet Union could not

Nuclear Power Plants Contain Many Layers of Safety

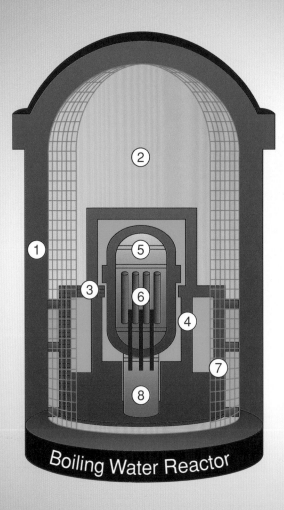

Boiling Water Reactor

1. **Shield Building Wall**
   · Three-foot thick reinforced concrete metal reinforcement
   · 2.5-inch diameter steel rods spaced one foot apart

2. **Containment Vessel**
   · 1.5-inch steel cylinder
   · 182 feet tall

3. **Dry Well Wall**
   · Metal reinforcement
   · 2.5-inch diameter steel rods spaced one foot apart
   · Five-foot thick reinforced concrete

4. **Bio Shield**
   · Four-foot thick leaded concrete with one-inch thick interior and exterior steel lining

5. **Reactor Vessel**

6. **Reactor Fuel**

7. **Weir Wall**
   · 1.5-foot thick concrete
   · 24 feet tall

8. **Pedestal**
   · Six-foot thick concrete with one-inch thick interior and exterior steel lining

Source: Nuclear Energy Commission.

happen in the United States. That basic design would not be licensed by the U.S. Nuclear Regulatory Commission. The Chernobyl reactor had no containment structure, so radioactivity did escape. The Chernobyl plant also had other design flaws. And safety systems that, at a minimum, could have reduced the severity of the accident had been ordered shut off while a test of plant equipment was conducted. Ukraine closed the last operating Chernobyl reactor in December 2000.

Safety Has Improved After the Three Mile Island Accident

The U.S. nuclear energy industry learned many lessons from the Three Mile Island accident near Harrisburg, Pa., in March 1979. Although it did not result in a single injury, the accident aroused public fears concerning nuclear safety.

Health experts concluded that the amount of radiation released into the atmosphere was too small to result in discernible direct health effects to the population in the vicinity of the plant. At least a dozen epidemiological studies conducted between 1981 and 1991 have borne this out.

The incident taught power plant operators a lot about how to improve reactor safety. According to the President's Commission on the Accident at Three Mile Island, headed by John G. Kemeny, the accident began with a single pump failure. As the operators addressed this rather routine problem, an important valve failed to work the way it was designed, causing a leak in the reactor's cooling system. More than two hours passed before the faulty valve was discovered and shut. During this time, thousands of gallons of radioactive water passed into the reactor building, but still within the containment. Some of the water was pumped to storage tanks in an auxiliary building, but these tanks quickly spilled over.

Meanwhile, the plant's operators were being misled by inadequately designed instrumentation that provided ambiguous indications of plant conditions. The operators believed the cooling system contained too much water, when in fact there was far too little. Because of this faulty reading, the operators took actions that essentially eliminated the system's ability to remove heat from the reactor core. Although the nuclear reaction had ceased, heat in the fuel continued to increase, causing the metal grid work and supports that hold the fuel in place to melt and, according to research commissioned by the U.S. Department of Energy, the pellets themselves began to disintegrate.

The impact of the accident on improved reactor safety was enormous. It led to greater understanding of potential risks, improved regulation, improved safety systems, and improved operator training and supervision. For instance, since Three Mile Island, U.S. nuclear power plant operators continually train on plant-specific simulators for accidents as well as routine operation.

Organizations Were Created to Monitor Nuclear Power Plants

In addition, the industry demonstrated a long-lasting commitment to safety and to excellence in nuclear power plant operation by establishing the Institute of Nuclear Power Operations. INPO, which is based in Atlanta, continues to examine the operation of all nuclear power plants in the United States and identifies any aspects that are not up to its standards of excellence. Its evaluations are important to all utilities, and all utilities work to achieve INPO's high standards. Another organization that was established in the aftermath of Three Mile Island—the National Academy for Nuclear Training—continues to check all plant design, testing, operations and training. All of this is in addition to strict regulation by the U.S. Nuclear Regulatory Commission.

Since the accident at Three Mile Island Unit 2, the remaining operating reactor (Unit 1) of that plant has achieved an extraordinary operating record. TMI-1, which was closed pending the outcome of extensive NRC hearings, remained off line for six years. It restarted in 1985 and began its climb to world-class performance immediately. For example, in 1989, TMI-1's capacity factor—a measure of reliability and safe operation—reached 100.03 percent, the best in the world. In cool weather, the plant can safely exceed its rated output and therefore boost

In May 1979 John Kemeny, chairman of a presidential commission investigating the accident at Three Mile Island, tours the control room at the facility.

its capacity factor above 100 percent. By 1991, TMI-1 set a world record for the longest operating cycle in the history of U.S. commercial energy: 479 consecutive days. In June 1997, TMI-1 completed the longest operating run of any light-water reactor worldwide: 616 days and 23 hours of continuous operation. The run also qualified as the longest of any steam-driven plant in the U.S., including fossil-fuel plants. And in September 1999, TMI-1 established its third world record of the decade, at 668 days of continuous operation. The plant's average capacity factor over the past five years is 96 percent, among the best in the world.

Nuclear Power Plants Are Vulnerable to Terrorist Attacks

Helmut Hirsch

After the terrorist attacks of September 11, 2001, experts have worried that the nation's nuclear power plants could be targeted by terrorists. The following selection is excerpted from a comprehensive critique of the nuclear power industry by Greenpeace International. Helmut Hirsch, the author, is an independent consultant in nuclear affairs living in Hanover, Germany. According to Hirsch, there are numerous reasons why a terrorist would target a nuclear power plant. Such an attack would release deadly radioactivity, he claims, and also disrupt the nation's power supply. The fact that such plants have been targeted by terrorists in the past indicates how attractive they are as targets, Hirsch contends.

Long before [the terrorist attacks of] September 11, 2001, numerous deliberate acts of terrorism have taken place in the 20th century. The terrorist threat appears to be particularly great, however, in the early 21st century. The overall situation, which is determined by economic, military, ideological and political factors, cannot be discussed and evaluated here.

It is important, however, to note the following: Although general attention is focussed on the threat from the direction of Islamic fundamentalism right now, there are, worldwide, many

Helmut Hirsch, Oda Becker, Mycle Schneider, Antony Froggatt, "D.1.I: Acts of Terrorism and War: Vulnerability of Nuclear Power Plants," *Nuclear Reactor Hazards*, April 2005, pp. 86–92. Reproduced by permission.

different ideological positions and organisations from which potential terrorists could be recruited. For example, the bombing of a building of the U.S. federal government in Oklahoma on April 19, 1995, which killed 169 people and injured more than 500, was committed by American extremists of the right. At present, the growing threat of Neo-Nazi terrorism in Germany also illustrates this point.

Nuclear Power Plants Are Prime Targets for Terrorism

There are numerous potential targets for terrorist attacks. Industrial installations, office buildings in city centres or filled sports stadia can appear "attractive", if a terrorist group plans to

A symbol of western power, this nuclear power plant in Guadalajara, Spain, could be an ideal target for terrorists.

CENTRAL NUCLEAR JOSE CABRERA

kill as many human beings as possible in one attack. A nuclear power plant (NPP), on the other hand, could be selected as a target for one of the following reasons, or a combination of those reasons:

- Because of the symbolic character—nuclear power can be seen as the epitome of technological development, as typical "high-tech". Furthermore, it is a technology of an ambiguous civilian/military nature. Many people therefore regard it as potentially very hazardous—justifiably so. Therefore, attacks against nuclear power plants can have a particularly strong psychological impact.
- Because of the long-term effect—an attack can lead to far-reaching radioactive contamination with long-lived radionuclides. The state that is being attacked will bear the mark of destruction for a long time. Furthermore, there will be economic damage for decades. Large areas (cities, industrial complexes) will have to be evacuated for an indefinite period, which could destabilize entire regions.
- Because of the immediate effects on the electricity generation in the region affected—nuclear power plants are, wherever they are operated, large and centralised components of the electricity supply system. The sudden shutdown of such a large plant can possibly lead to a collapse of the local electricity grid.
- Because of the longer-term effects on electricity generation, not only in the affected region, but also in other regions (possibly even in all states where nuclear power plants are operated)—a successful attack against a nuclear power plant in one country is also an attack against all nuclear power plants in the world. After such an attack has demonstrated the vulnerability of an NPP, it is possible that other NPPs will be shut down in the country affected, but also in other countries.

Reasons Terrorists Might Not Attack a Nuclear Power Plant

There are also conceivable reasons, from the point of view of a terrorist group, against a nuclear power plant as a target: A

FBI officials survey the damage after a 1993 terrorist bomb damaged the parking garage at the World Trade Center in New York City.

nuclear installation can be less vulnerable than other targets; radiological damage could occur in large distances in non-enemy countries; and the attacked country could react with extreme violence. There seems to be no chance, however, to estimate probabilities that certain targets would be attacked, or not. It is clear and undisputed that a terror attack against a nuclear power plant is possible; and also, that there are many types of other targets for such attacks as well.

Terror-attacks against nuclear power plants can be performed with a large variety of means. It is not possible to list all conceivable scenarios since it is absolutely impossible to anticipate all products of human fantasy. Since September 11, 2001, authorities have been focussing on airplane suicide attacks. However, totally different scenarios are also plausible.

In principle, attacks can vary with respect to the means being used, the concrete target, the organisation, number and effort of the attackers as well as other factors. For each of those variables, there are many possibilities of implementation. Even the attempt to completely list what is foreseeable therefore would lead to a matrix with a large number of different scenarios.

Therefore, some examples only will be presented here, to show the diversity of the threat. Those examples will include scenarios that, so far, have hardly received attention in the expert and public debates.

Nuclear Power Plants Have Already Been Targeted

Terror attacks against nuclear plants are not purely theoretical. In the past, a number of such attacks have already taken place. Luckily, they did not lead to a catastrophic radioactive release so far. A few examples can illustrate the record:

- On 12 November 1972, three hijackers took control of a DC-9 of Southern Airlines and threatened to crash it on the Oak Ridge military nuclear research reactor. The hijackers flew on to Cuba after they obtained two million dollars.
- December 1977: Basque separatists set off bombs damaging the reactor vessel and a steam generator and killing two workers at the Lemoniz NPP under construction in Spain.
- December 1982: [African National Congress] fighters set off four bombs inside the Koeberg plant under construction in South Africa, despite tight security.
- May 1986: Three of the four off-site power lines leading to the Palo Verde NPP in Arizona were sabotaged by short-circuiting.
- February 1993: At Three Mile Island NPP (Pennsylvania), a man crashed his station wagon through the security gate and rammed the vehicle under a partly opened door in the turbine building. Security guards found him hiding in that building four hours later.
- In 1993, the terrorists behind the car bombing against the World Trade Centre, belonging to the terrorist networks that claimed to be part of the Islamic jihad, threatened to target nuclear sites in a letter received by the *New York Times* and

authenticated by the authorities. In addition, the investigation is said to have revealed that the terrorist group trained in November 1992 in a camp near Harrisburg, in Pennsylvania 15 km [kilometers] away from the Three Mile Island nuclear power station.

- November 1994: Bomb threat at Ignalina NPP, Lithuania. However, no explosion occurred and no bomb was found in the power plant. . . .

A Nuclear Power Plant Offers Multiple Targets

Of all nuclear plants and other facilities with toxic inventories, such as chemical factories, nuclear power plants are probably the most "attractive" targets for terrorist or military attacks. They are wide-spread (at least in a number of industrialized countries), contain a considerable radioactive inventory and are, as already pointed out, important components of the electricity supply system. Furthermore, they are large buildings with a typical structure, visible even over large distances.

The area of a nuclear power plant consists of several tens of thousands of square meters. The core piece of the installation is the reactor building, which, as the name indicates, contains the reactor with the highly radioactive nuclear fuel (in the order of magnitude of 100 tonnes), as well as important cooling and safety systems.

It is likely that the reactor building will be the primary target in case of an attack. If the reactor is operating as the attack occurs, and if the cooling is interrupted, a core melt can result within a very short time (about 1 hour). Even if the reactor is shut

ANOTHER OPINION

Nuclear Power Plants Were Not Designed to Thwart 9/11-Type Attacks

Nuclear "reactors have the most robust engineering of any buildings in the civil sector. . . . They are designed to be earthquake-proof, and our experiences in California and Japan have shown them to be so. They are also built to withstand impacts, but not that of a wide-bodied passenger jet full of fuel. A deliberate hit of that sort is something that was never in any scenario at the design stage. These are vulnerable targets and the consequences of a direct hit could be catastrophic."

David Kyd, quoted in "Vulnerability of U.S. Power Plants to Terrorist Attack and Internal Sabotage," Physicians for Social Responsibility, www.psr.org.

down, the decay heat is still considerable, and the fuel will also melt—although somewhat slower.

In case of destruction of the reactor building with failure of the cooling systems, a core melt accident of the most hazardous category results: Rapid melting with open containment. The resulting radioactive releases will be particularly high, and occur particularly early.

Spent fuel elements, glowing an eerie blue while submerged in a special tank at a French nuclear plant, are vulnerable to terrorist attacks.

The spent fuel storage pool is another vulnerable component with considerable radioactive inventory. In some plants, it can contain several times the amount of fuel (and thus more long-lived radioactive substances) than the reactor core itself. In some nuclear power plants, this pool is located inside the containment and is protected against external impacts by a concrete hull (for example in German pressurized water reactors). In many cases, however, the pool is installed in a separate building with less protection (this applies to many U.S. nuclear power plants). The pool in German boiling water reactors of generation 69 is located inside the reactor building, but above the containment, and protected to a considerably lesser degree than the reactor. . . .

In the following, various possibilities for terror attacks on NPPs are listed, as examples. Almost all of them could also take place in times of war, committed by commando troops or a fifth column. Some of the scenarios could be implemented, with minor changes, in the course of military operations.

Attack from the air:
- Deliberate crash of commercial airliner, freight plane or one or several business jets (possibly loaded with explosives)
- Deliberate crash of a helicopter loaded with explosives, or dropping a bomb from helicopter
- Attack by military plane (with bombs and/or other weapons), possibly combined with deliberate crash of military plane
- Deliberate crash of a pilot-less aircraft (drone) loaded with explosives

Attack from the water:
- Crash of boat loaded with explosives into cooling water intake structures from sea or river
- Deliberate explosion of gas tanker close to NPP

Firing on plant from a distance:
- Shelling with field howitzer, with explosive grenades (from ground or water)
- Firing with armour-piercing weapons (rockets), from ground, water or from the air

Intrusion of attackers onto plant area:
- Use of one or more car bomb(s)

- Intrusion of armed attackers, carrying explosives, from land or water
- Intrusion of armed attackers, carrying explosives, by helicopter or ultralight aircraft

Attacks involving insiders:

- Insiders support attack from outside, for example through creation of confusion, obstruction of counter measures or simultaneous attack from inside
- Explosives are being smuggled on the site and into buildings; are exploded in safety-relevant sectors
- A knowledgeable group of insiders directly intervenes in the operation of the plant, triggering a severe accident
- Insiders perform sabotage during repair and maintenance
- Armed members of the security personnel perform an attack from the inside or support an attack from outside

Attacks against installations located outside the plant perimeter:

- Attack against the cooling water intake building of a nuclear power plant from the water (with boats, possibly divers), using explosives
- Attack against the grid connection of a nuclear power plant (or other nuclear plants), for example by blowing up power connections, and against on-site power supply (emergency diesels etc.)

Nuclear Power Plants Are Safe from Terrorist Attacks

U.S. Nuclear Regulatory Commission

This selection summarizes the role played by the U.S. Nuclear Regulatory Commission (NRC) in tightening security at nuclear power plants after the September 11, 2001, terrorist attacks. According to the NRC, which is charged with overseeing the nation's nuclear power facilities, safeguarding the country's nuclear power plants from terrorist attacks is one of its top concerns. The NRC works with the Department of Homeland Security and other federal and state agencies to ensure that nuclear power generation is safely conducted.

Since the accident at Three Mile Island in 1979, NRC [Nuclear Regulatory Commission] has heightened its regulatory oversight and made sweeping changes in emergency response planning and nuclear power plant operations. Over the years since that accident, the NRC has responded to domestic radiological events and security matters, overseen licensees' emergency preparedness, and supported and coordinated with other Federal, State and local response organizations. The NRC has also maintained staff on-call and around-the-clock at the NRC Headquarters Operations Center. These actions have been performed in coordination with other Federal agencies under the NRC's Incident Response Plan and Federal Radiological Emergency Response Plan (FRERP). For more than 20 years,

"Protecting Our Nation Since 9-11-01," *U.S. Nuclear Regulatory Commission*, 2004.

the NRC, in conjunction with the Federal Emergency Management Agency, has conducted a comprehensive emergency exercise program with NRC licensees. This program includes participation by State and local response organizations and other agencies of the Federal government.

Security Has Tightened Since 9/11

As a result of the attacks on September 11, 2001, the NRC has increased its focus on potential terrorist scenarios as initiating events in emergency preparedness. It should be noted that NRC's response to a radiological release—whether caused by a terrorist attack, equipment malfunction, or natural disaster—could be similar, even though each type of event may have unique concerns. As part of the Orders issued in February 2002, nuclear power plant operators were required to make enhancements in several areas of emergency preparedness, including emergency response facilities, emergency response organizations, classification of and response to credible threats, and evaluation of a broader range of hazards. Nuclear industry groups and Federal, State, and local government agencies assisted in the prompt implementation of these measures and participated in drills and exercises to test new planning elements. Since that time, the NRC has reviewed licensee commitments to address these requirements and verified the implementation by direct inspection.

As part of the NRC's transitional . . . exercises at nuclear power plants, the NRC is evaluating the licensees' emergency preparedness response concurrent with their security response. Licensees have improved their emergency preparedness response capabilities through the identification of areas for improvement during these exercises. Licensees have also shared lessons learned with other licensees, States, and local response organizations.

In addition, the NRC conducted a formal evaluation of the emergency preparedness planning basis in view of the threat environment that has existed since the terrorist attacks on September 11, 2001. This evaluation addressed all aspects of nuclear power plant emergency preparedness requirements. In doing so, the evaluation determined that emergency preparedness at nuclear power plants remains strong, but identified several areas for improvement. These areas included communications processes, resource management issues, drill program enhancements, and changes to NRC guidance documents used by licensees. The NRC is currently reviewing and inspecting these improvements. Additionally, the NRC recognizes the

This nuclear power plant operator at Palo Verde goes through a checklist as part of a daily security regimen.

An instrument panel in a simulated control room at a nuclear plant is used for training in a variety of emergency scenarios.

importance of bolstering communication of its emergency preparedness activities with internal and external stakeholders including the public, the industry, the international nuclear community, as well as Federal, State and local government agencies. The NRC continues to emphasize the importance of emergency preparedness to mitigate the effects of potential security threats and other events.

The NRC Is Well Equipped to Handle Emergency

As part of the overall improvement of emergency response capabilities, the NRC has improved the Headquarters Operations Center, where the NRC directs emergency response activities. The NRC Operations Center is continually staffed with knowledgeable personnel, who have the expertise and ability to evaluate events and alert NRC management, other Federal partners, and licensees, as necessary, about unfolding events. The NRC has added secure video teleconferencing in the Operations Center, as well as increased the capacity for secure communications and classified information storage. In the four NRC Regional offices, the Regional Incident Response Centers also have similarly undergone substantial improvements, including additional space and improved communications capability. The NRC also continues to improve coordination with other Federal agencies to refine Federal plans for response to an emergency or terrorist event involving nuclear materials or facilities. NRC actively takes part in Federal interagency exercises such as the Top Officials (TOPOFF) series to test and improve these plans.

The NRC is also playing an active role in enhancing Federal, State, and private sector incident response capabilities for nuclear and radiological emergencies and incidents. With the passage of the Homeland Security Act of 2002, the DHS has been vested with the overall responsibility for coordinating the Federal response to domestic incidents. The NRC has been actively working with DHS to develop and administer a National Incident Management System (NIMS) and National Response Plan (NRP) consistent with Homeland Security Presidential Directive 5 (Management of Domestic Incidents). The NRC, along with other Federal agencies, and NRC licensees regularly participate in exercises involving NRC licensed facilities. The NRC is also committed to greater use of security scenarios in exercises, such as the scenario used in the June 2004 exercise at Indian Point nuclear power plant. This commitment is not new to the NRC. The

ANOTHER OPINION

Nuclear Power Plants Are Too Robust to Be Vulnerable to Terrorism

Various studies have looked at [attacks similar to those that occurred on September 11, 2001] on nuclear power plants. They show that nuclear reactors would be more resistant to such attacks than virtually any other civil installation. A thorough study was undertaken by the U.S. Electric Power Research Institute using specialist consultants and paid for by the U.S. Department of Energy. It concludes that US reactor structures "are robust and would protect the fuel from impacts of large commercial aircraft."

Uranium Information Centre Ltd., "Safety of Nuclear Power Reactors: Paper 14," May 2006. www.uic.com.au.

agency began to use security scenarios long before the September 11 terrorist attacks as illustrated by a drill involving considerable FBI field participation which was conducted at Palo Verde nuclear power plant in 2000. Additional information on the NRC's emergency response exercises is presented later in this document.

A safety official measures radiation levels during a simulated terrorist response drill conducted by the Nuclear Regulatory Commission.

With respect to planning for Continuity of Operations (COOP), the NRC has accelerated infrastructure enhancements at our alternative COOP site, tested backup capabilities, conducted an agency-wide COOP exercise, and participated in a National COOP exercise in May 2004. The NRC's COOP and Continuity of Government (COG) plans have been in place well before the terrorist attacks in 2001. In the future, the NRC expects to fully exercise the agency and national-level COOP capabilities to ensure readiness against potential terrorist attacks or other incidents that could disrupt operations. Additionally, the NRC plans to continue to participate in future COG exercises that enhance preparedness for the agency and the Nation.

When the NRC supplemented the DBTs [Design Basis Threat] in April 2003, the agency began discussing with DHS, the White House Security Council, FBI, DoD [Department of Defense], and other agencies the potential need for an "integrated response" by government assets to help defend against threats that could exceed the DBTs. The concept of "integrated response" applies to both prevention of and response to a potential terrorist event. The NRC has a strong history related to the integration of responders, in both exercises and actual events and the agency is actively engaged in both prevention or deterrence and response elements of integrated response planning.

The NRC also continues to have an active role in a number of DHS initiatives to further prepare our Nation against potential terrorist attacks. In particular, NRC involvement includes participation in a number of Homeland Security Council policy coordinating committees, the Deputies Committee, the Federal Radiological Preparedness Coordinating Committee, the Federal Response Plan's Emergency Support Function Leaders Group, numerous Federal interagency working groups (including development of the National Infrastructure Protection Plan), and NRC-initiated outreach activities with industry groups and State agencies. The NRC will continue to strengthen our partnerships with other Federal agencies to implement a national framework for domestic incident response.

5

Nuclear Waste Is a Serious Problem

Harvey Blatt

Harvey Blatt is a professor of geology at the Institute of Earth Sciences at Hebrew University of Jerusalem. He is also the author of six textbooks. In the following selection Blatt outlines the dangers associated with nuclear toxic waste. He notes that the fuel rod assemblies used in plants must be replaced every eighteen to twenty-four months. The result is a huge stockpile of spent rods, which are highly radioactive. At present this waste is stored at nuclear power plants, but the federal government is obligated to provide a permanent storage facility. Blatt contends, however, that no permanent off-site storage facility has been approved, leaving waste in temporary, unsafe storage.

T he operation of America's nuclear power plants over the past 40 years has left us with [a] monstrous problem, and this one is still growing. What can we do with the mountains of nuclear-waste products that America's nuclear research, weapons program, and power plants have generated? Some of it will remain dangerous and potentially lethal for thousands to millions of years—that is, forever as far as the human species is concerned. More than half of all Americans live within 75 miles of an above-ground waste storage site.

Harvey Blatt, *America's Environmental Report Card*, Cambridge, MA: MIT Press, 2005. Reproduced by permission of the MIT Press, Cambridge, MA.

Most Radioactive Waste Originates at Nuclear Power Plants

Radioactive waste is classified for convenience as either low-level or high-level. Ninety-nine percent of all radioactive waste is low-level, meaning it will remain significantly radioactive and dangerous for *only* 300–500 years. In these wastes the maximum level of radioactivity is up to 1,000 times the amount considered acceptable in the environment. About 63 percent of this waste (but 94 percent of the radioactivity) originates in nuclear power plants. The rest comes from hospitals (cancer

Steel-encased drums containing low-level radioactive waste lie scattered in a trench at a nuclear waste facility.

treatment), university and industrial laboratories (research), manufacturing (measurement), and military facilities (nuclear-weapons manufacturing and research). The range of materials in low-level waste is wide, and includes fabric, metal, plastic, glass, paper, wood, and animal remains.

Low-level wastes are usually sealed in metal drums, commonly after being burned in special incinerators to reduce their volume, and either stored aboveground in vast "holding pens," or buried in shallow trenches beneath about 3 feet of soil. In principle, the storage site should be carefully chosen with respect to the location and geology to ensure that there is no contamination of plants, soils, and groundwater. In practice, the metal drums corrode over time, and stress is placed on them by the continuous radiation from the material in the drums. Many drums at some sites have leaked radioactive liquids into the soil and groundwater.

Better Solutions Are Needed to Store Toxic Waste

Clearly, a safer method for storage of these drums is needed. The safest method is to store them in excavations tens of feet deep but far above the groundwater table in arid or semiarid areas of the Western United States. This method would keep water from the drums, and the waste could be easily and continuously monitored for a few centuries until it was no longer hazardous and could be landfilled.

Under congressional mandate, regional compacts that include several adjacent states have been established to store low-level waste on a regional rather than a local basis. There will be one storage site for each compact except for the Rocky Mountain compact, which will use the site of the Northwest compact at Hanford, Washington. Ten such compacts have been established, but only two compacts have settled on a storage site. However, lawsuits have been filed by environmental groups against some of the host states, and some compact states have recently withdrawn from their compact because of disagreements with other states in the compact. The future of the

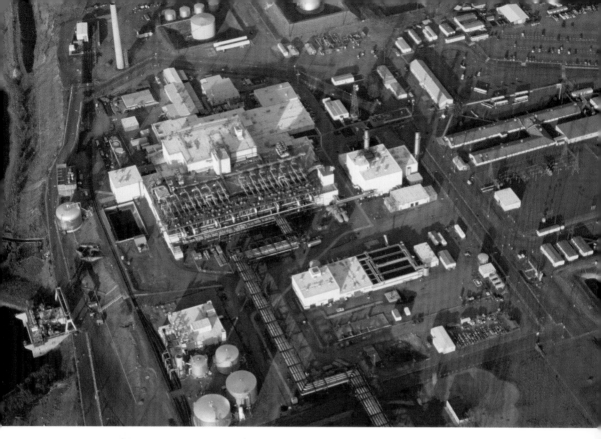

This is an aerial view of the Hanford nuclear site in eastern Washington, the location of a new compact.

compacts is uncertain. Most low-level waste is still stored at the places where it was produced.

Another disposal method for low-level waste has been to cast it into concrete, encased in steel drums, and dump it into the deep ocean. Tens of thousands of tons of such wastes have been dumped at an internationally agreed site in the Atlantic Ocean 1,300 miles southwest of England. The concrete ensures that the waste will reach the floor of the ocean 15,000 feet down intact, where it is supposed to remain safe and undisturbed for at least hundreds of years. The concept is that any leakage over time would be diluted by the vast mass of ocean water and dispersed harmlessly into the surroundings. The problem with this approach is that as the drums begin to leak, a process that may already have begun, the fish that swim nearby become irradiated. When the smaller fish are eaten by larger fish the effects of

In Nevada a worker walks in a tunnel deep inside Yucca Mountain, the controversial proposed storage facility for nuclear waste.

the irradiation are spread in an ever-widening circle whose end is unclear. But it cannot be good. The best we can hope for is an insignificant effect. Our experiments with nuclear-waste disposal continue. . . .

Storage of High Level Waste Is Political

High-level radioactive waste is a by-product of nuclear-weapons production and commercial reactors. It consists of spent fuel rods and liquid materials involved in reprocessing spent fuel to recover highly radioactive plutonium, and was produced at more than 100 former U.S. nuclear-weapons sites. High-level waste will be dangerously radioactive forever—that is, for at least tens of thousands of years. One estimate of their toxicity suggests that less than 1 gallon of the waste would be enough to bring every person in the world to the danger level for radiation exposure if it were evenly distributed. There are now about 100 million gallons in storage at 158 sites in 40 states. Sweden, Finland, Japan, and Switzerland are the only countries that have succeeded in having repository sites for high-level waste accepted by their citizens. The United States is in the final stages of establishing a site.

There are over 158 nuclear waste storage sights in the U.S.

In 1982 Congress required the federal government to find a suitable site for storing the nation's ever-growing accumulation of high-level nuclear waste. In 1987 the Department of Energy settled on Yucca Mountain, 87 miles northwest of Las Vegas, Nevada. Feasibility studies have cost $4 billion. As of 2001, the facility itself is projected to cost $57.5 billion, up 26 percent from the estimate made by the Department of Energy only 3 years earlier. Movement of high-level waste from the present 131 storage sites in 39 states to Yucca Mountain was set to begin in 1985. But because of lawsuits by the State of Nevada and other groups opposed to the site, the opening was pushed back to 1989, then 1998, then 2003, and as of this writing the date is 2010. Few would bet on 2010 being the final date. Current (2002) Nevada governor Kenny Guinn said of the federal government's decision to use Yucca Mountain, "This decision stinks, the whole process stinks and we'll see him in court." With many lawsuits pending,

"Nuclear Energy Baby," cartoon by Bill Deore. Copyright © *The Dallas Morning News* 1986. Reproduced by permission.

Nevada state official Robert Loux said, "I think we can keep them out of the site for decades."

In the meantime, high-level waste continues to accumulate at the nation's reactors. Companies claim that their storage areas are full or nearly full and demand immediate action from the federal government. The current terrorist threat has increased the urgency of their demands. To transport the high-level waste to Yucca Mountain, more than 150,000 shipments of vitrified waste through 45 states would be made over 30 years, 3,000–4,000 shipments per year. That's about 10 shipments per day, 365 days a year, for 30 years. Transportation would be by road, rail, and canal, and would pass through or close to many highly populated regions. This effort has been dubbed "Mobile Chernobyl" by the media and Yucca Mountain's opponents, a catchy but inaccurate phrase that sends shudders down a sane person's spine. Since 9/11, Americans have become aware that trucks and trains carrying nuclear waste are tempting terrorist targets. Of course, the transportation problem will be similar for any storage site. It brings to mind the well-known expression about being caught between a rock and a hard place.

The nuclear industry projects it will produce more than the Yucca Mountain capacity of 77,000 tons before 2020. This is an estimate for the waste produced by industry and does not include storage space for 2,500 tons of waste from military reactors and untold tons of glassified radioactive liquid wastes stored at former bomb plants. There has been no search for a second site, despite the fact that the first site is already oversubscribed. The federal government is still fighting with opponents of the first site. At present, high-level waste is stored "temporarily" at 130 nuclear power plants and military installations. Eventually it will have to be moved *somewhere*.

Nuclear Waste Is Not a Serious Problem

Nuclear Energy Institute

This selection, prepared by the Nuclear Energy Institute, an industry trade association, details the extraordinary measures taken to safely store radioactive waste from nuclear power plants. As the NEI contends, spent nuclear fuel is stored safely at power plants around the country. The spent fuel is carefully monitored, and many safety procedures are used to ensure that no radioactivity is released into the atmosphere. The NEI claims that the federal government is committed to building a long-term storage facility at Yucca Mountain in Nevada, which will provide even safer storage for spent nuclear fuel.

Today, more than 100 nuclear power plants generate 20 percent of the electricity in the United States—without producing any air emissions.

A byproduct of nuclear energy is radioactive used nuclear fuel. The U.S. nuclear energy industry has safely managed used fuel for decades, carefully containing it from the environment. Ultimately, when the federal government takes responsibility for this material, as required by law, the U.S. Department of Energy will continue the safe management of used nuclear fuel at a federal facility.

What Is Used Nuclear Fuel?

To generate electricity, nuclear power plants use uranium oxide. This solid fuel—in the form of small ceramic pellets—is placed

Nuclear Energy institute, "Safely Managing Used Nuclear Fuel," Washington, DC: Nuclear Energy Institute, 2003. Reproduced by Permission.

inside metal fuel rods and grouped into bundles called fuel assemblies.

Fission involves the splitting of uranium atoms in a chain reaction. This produces a tremendous amount of heat energy that is used to boil water into steam. That steam, in turn, drives a turbine generator to produce electricity, distributed across power lines to homes, businesses and schools.

Over time, the energy in a nuclear plant's fuel is consumed, and every 18–24 months the plant is shut down, and the oldest fuel assemblies are removed and replaced by new ones.

Those assemblies, in the process of generating enormous amounts of energy, have become intensely radioactive as a result

Specially reinforced cylinders like this one will be used inside Yucca Mountain for storing highly radioactive nuclear waste.

of the fission process. Contrary to images in fictional movies or television programs, trained workers safely store and carefully manage this used fuel at the plant sites. It is solid and compact, and relatively small in volume.

Plants Can Safely Store Used Fuel for Decades

Most plants store used fuel in steel-lined, concrete vaults filled with water. In this manner, the water acts as a natural barrier for radiation from the fuel assemblies.

The water also keeps the fuel cool while the radiation decays—or becomes less radioactive. The water itself does not leave the inside of the power plant's concrete building.

Nuclear power plants were originally designed to store at least a decade's worth of used fuel. However, many plants already have run out of used fuel pool capacity. The Nuclear Waste Policy Act of 1982 requires the federal government to begin moving used fuel from plant sites in 1998, but it has not yet fulfilled this obligation to begin managing used fuel at a federal facility.

Given current progress at the Yucca Mountain site [in Nevada], designated as the nation's permanent repository for used fuel, the government may not begin to remove used fuel before the facility opens or is near completion—sometime after 2010.

Safety and Security Are Integral to Fuel Storage Systems

Above-ground storage systems—like used fuel pools—incorporate a number of security features to protect public health and safety.

The foremost safety feature is the robust container itself: steel or steel-reinforced concrete, 18 or more inches thick. The containers are extremely rugged, using materials like steel, concrete and lead that also serve as a proven, effective radiation shield. Each container—depending on the design—can hold up to 68 12-foot-long used fuel assemblies. Once loaded, plants store the containers hor-

At a French nuclear plant, spent nuclear fuel rods sit in an immersion tank, an example of above-ground nuclear storage.

izontally in a concrete vault, or stand them upright on a three-foot-thick concrete pad. In 2004, companies were using nearly 530 of these containers safely at U.S. nuclear plant sites.

The makers of dry storage containers design and test the containers to ensure they prevent the release of radioactivity, even under the most extreme conditions—earthquakes, tornadoes, hurricanes, floods and sabotage. All of the designs use natural cooling, and require no mechanical devices.

Dry storage containers, like all nuclear plant buildings, are well-protected from a potential terrorist attack, whether ground-based or airborne. In tests conducted by EPRI, a Palo Alto, Calif.-based research firm, dry storage containers proved highly resistant to the impact of a commercial aircraft, as well as difficult targets to strike.

A truck transports containers of nuclear waste to an underground processing plant in New Mexico.

Used Fuel Management Preserves Nuclear Energy Benefits

At each of America's nuclear power plants, public health and safety are paramount—from the plants' design with multiple barriers and backup operating systems to continual training and testing of the people who run the plants.

Nuclear power plants are the nation's largest source of emission-free electricity. No other source of electricity in the United States contributes such a large share of energy production while having such a limited environmental impact.

Just as important—as America's second-leading source of electricity—U.S. nuclear plants play a significant role in improving people's lives—whether it's powering offices and factories or providing electricity for a digital economy.

Plant operators are committed to manage the nation's used nuclear fuel safely and responsibly until the federal government opens a centralized repository. Doing so not only protects public health and safety, it also ensures that Americans can enjoy the benefits of reliable economical and emission-free nuclear energy.

The canister storage building at the Hanford, Washington, nuclear facility sits above underground vaults which hold spent fuel waste.

Centralized Storage Will Hold Down Costs

While the use of above-ground, dry storage allows the nation's nuclear power plants to continue providing reliable, economical and emission-free electricity to millions of Americans, a centralized facility is still required.

Nuclear power plants—while carefully and safely managing used fuel for more than four decades—were never built for long-term storage. Experts agree that moving used fuel to a single facility—built specifically for that purpose—will reduce the cost to the public while improving on an already excellent safety record. The U.S. Department of Energy is developing such a facility at Yucca Mountain, Nevada.

Until the centralized facility opens, the industry will continue to use dry storage systems subject to the same rigorous safety standards and regulatory oversight as every other aspect of nuclear power plant operations.

Another factor in favor of centralized storage is that dry storage systems are expensive. Depending on the design, a container's cost can range from $500,000 to more than $1 million. Some nuclear plants will need dozens of these containers until the federal government opens the Yucca mountain facility after 2010. Consumers of nuclear-generated electricity will have to foot the bill for these on-site storage systems, despite the fact the Nuclear Waste Policy Act never envisioned the need for on-site storage.

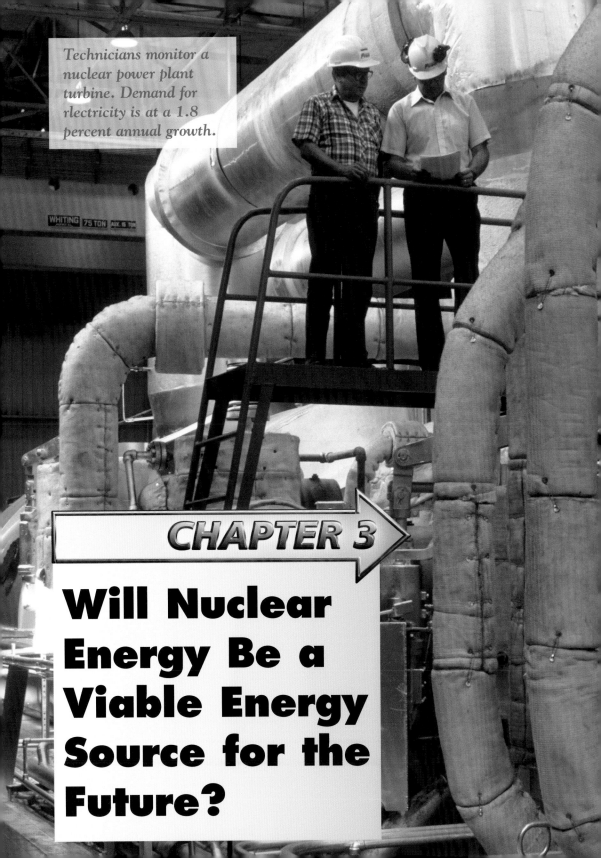

Technicians monitor a nuclear power plant turbine. Demand for rlectricity is at a 1.8 percent annual growth.

CHAPTER 3

Will Nuclear Energy Be a Viable Energy Source for the Future?

America Needs Nuclear Power

Nuclear Energy Institute

As an advocate for the nuclear industry, the Nuclear Energy Institute maintains that nuclear power has an important role to play in providing affordable energy to the United States. This article notes that all energy sources have advantages and disadvantages. As energy demand grows, nuclear power will play an important role in meeting that demand. The article asserts that nuclear fuel is relatively affordable and plentiful compared to other energy sources. It is not subject to disruptions as were seen when Hurricane Katrina halted natural gas production in September 2005. The article also notes the broader acceptance that nuclear power has today, even among people who formerly opposed it.

Nuclear Energy Is Critical to Reliable U.S. Energy Supply

Nuclear energy produces electricity for one in five U.S. homes and businesses. The 103 nuclear power plants in 31 states have made tremendous efficiency gains over the past dozen years, increasing their electricity production by one-third to 789 billion kilowatt-hours in 2004.

The U.S. Department of Energy, in its energy outlook for 2005, forecasts growth in electricity demand of 1.8 percent annually through 2025. To satisfy that demand, DOE predicts the United States must increase electricity production by nearly 50 percent—the equivalent of adding more than 250 new

Nuclear Energy Institute, "U.S. Needs New Nuclear Plants to Meet Energy Demand, Maintain Supply Diversity," Washington, DC: Nuclear Energy Institute, 2005.

1,000-megawatt power plants. DOE's demand growth projection is a conservative estimate and is below the actual growth rate of the last five decades.

Along with coal-fired power plants, nuclear power plants are the workhorses of the U.S. electricity system, and they can help meet the growth in electricity demand resulting from a growing U.S. economy and population. But that is just one of the many benefits of nuclear energy.

A tanker vessel sits at a floating liquid natural gas facility in Chesapeake Bay on the U.S. eastern seaboard.

Nuclear Energy Helps Maintain Energy Diversity

A diverse mix of energy sources enables America to balance the cost of electricity production, availability and environmental impacts to our best advantage. The United States produces electricity from a mix of different fuels. Coal and nuclear energy are the foundation of the U.S. electricity supply system, representing 50 percent and 20 percent of U.S. electricity supply, respectively. The rest comes from natural gas-fired power plants, hydroelectric dams and small amounts of renewable energy.

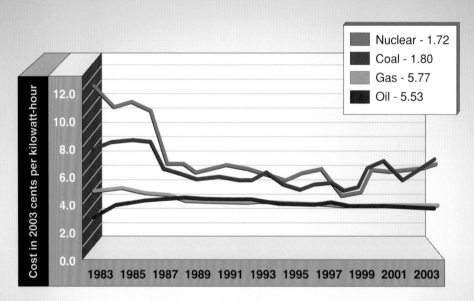

U.S. Electricity Production Costs

Legend:
- Nuclear - 1.72
- Coal - 1.80
- Gas - 5.77
- Oil - 5.53

Y-axis: Cost in 2003 cents per kilowatt-hour (0.0, 2.0, 4.0, 6.0, 8.0, 10.0, 12.0)

X-axis: 1983 1985 1987 1989 1991 1993 1995 1997 1999 2001 2003

Electricity generated from nuclear plants is the most reliable, affordable baseload electricity source. And unlike other fuel sources, such as natural gas, nuclear energy is not subject to dramatic swings in fuel prices.

Source: Federal Energy Regulatory Commission, FERC.

This diversity of fuels is one of the great strengths of the U.S. electric supply system. Each source of electricity has unique advantages and disadvantages, and each has its place in a balanced electricity supply portfolio.

Natural gas-fired electricity generation has more than doubled since 1990 to 18 percent of all production. Nearly all power plants built over the past 15 years are fueled by natural gas. However, natural gas is subject to significant price fluctuations because it also is used as a heating fuel and in industrial processes. Natural gas supplies have tightened considerably, driving up prices. The greater the country's reliance on natural gas, the greater the likelihood that electricity prices will experience increased volatility in the future.

Storms Can Disrupt Some Energy Sources

Such energy supply vulnerabilities were self-evident in August and September 2005, when Hurricanes Katrina and Rita struck the energy-rich Gulf Coast, disrupting natural gas supplies across the nation. "It is clear that when you're dependent upon natural gas and/or hydrocarbons to fuel your economy and that supply gets disrupted, we need alternative sources of energy," President Bush said following the disasters. "And that's why I believe so strongly in nuclear power."

"We can't expect to reduce air pollution without reliable nuclear energy," Sen. Tom Carper (D-Del.) said. "Nuclear power significantly reduces our dependence on natural gas for electricity generation, while at the same time reducing harmful emissions of carbon dioxide that lead to global warming."

In addition, over-reliance on natural gas could have dire consequences for the nation's energy security. The vast majority of exporters of natural gas are nations that have proved unstable over time as America's sources of imported oil.

By comparison, the uranium fuel for U.S. nuclear plants is abundant, readily available from reliable allies such as Canada and Australia and low in cost. The low fuel cost, coupled with industry success over the last 15 years in reducing operating costs, makes America's 103 nuclear energy plants among the lowest-cost sources of electricity available. Once built, new nuclear power plants would provide the same degree of price stability for consumers.

Prudent energy planning demands a balanced approach—one in which all fuels play an appropriate role. These include coal, nuclear energy, natural gas, hydro, and renewables such as solar and wind power.

Nuclear Energy Has Clean-Air Benefits

Approximately 30 percent of U.S. electricity supply is produced at emission-free power plants—hydroelectric, nuclear energy and renewables. Nuclear energy represents 73 percent of this emission-free electricity generation.

The electricity produced by nuclear power plants displaces electricity that would otherwise be supplied by oil-, gas- or coal-fired generating capacity. Hence, nuclear energy plays a vital role in our national air quality compliance programs.

In 2004, nuclear power plants prevented the emission of about 3.4 million tons of sulfur dioxide and 1.1 million tons of smog-causing nitrogen oxide—pollutants controlled by the Clean Air Act.

Nuclear plants also prevented the discharge of about 700 million metric tons of carbon dioxide into the atmosphere in 2004. This amount equals the carbon dioxide released from nearly all U.S. passenger cars combined.

In April 2005, a Polestar Applied Technology study, commissioned by NEI, concluded that the nine northeastern states cooperating on the Regional Greenhouse Gas Initiative would be incapable of meeting their ambitious goals to cap carbon emissions without the help of the region's 15 nuclear power plants. Without those plants, the region would be forced to generate about 50 percent of its electricity from natural gas in order to meet their carbon cap goals.

The environmental benefits of nuclear energy are gaining greater recognition. In recent years, the Massachusetts Institute of Technology, Harvard University and the Earth Institute at New York's Columbia University have released studies advocating expanded use of nuclear energy to combat global climate change.

Environmentalists also advocate the expanded use of nuclear power to meet our planet's energy needs while protecting our environment. Greenpeace founder Patrick Moore said in January that nuclear energy is "the only non-greenhouse gas-emitting power source that can effectively replace fossil fuels and satisfy global demand."

British scientist James Lovelock, a leading international environmentalist, wrote in the British newspaper *The Independent* that if we are serious about combating the threat of global warming while meeting rising electricity demand, "nuclear power is the only green solution."

Counterculture icon Stewart Brand and founder of the Whole Earth Catalog, called for a reassessment of America's use of nuclear energy. "The only technology ready to fill the gap

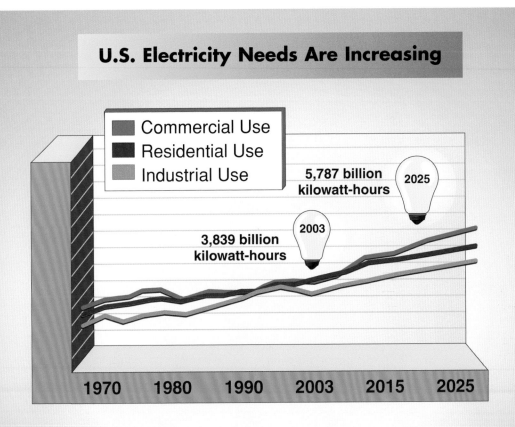

U.S. Electricity Needs Are Increasing

Commercial Use
Residential Use
Industrial Use

5,787 billion kilowatt-hours — 2025

3,839 billion kilowatt-hours — 2003

1970   1980   1990   2003   2015   2025

Source: U.S. Department of Energy.

and stop carbon dioxide loading of the atmosphere is nuclear power," Brand wrote in the MIT Technology Review.

Linking Energy, Environmental Policy

Looking to the future, U.S. energy and environmental policy require that our nation maintain at least the current 30 percent share of non-emitting electric generating capacity if the nation is to meet its clean air goals.

Even with conservative assumptions about increases in electricity demand, and assuming a doubling of renewable energy production, the United States will be challenged to maintain the current proportion of emission-free electricity production without a substantial increase in nuclear energy.

Plumes of steam escape from the cooling towers of this coal-fired power plant in Maryland.

Comprehensive energy policy legislation enacted in 2005 provides limited incentives to jump-start new reactor construction, just as similar legislation has done for wind and other power technologies. These include loan-guarantees for energy-neutral technologies, including nuclear and renewables; production tax credits (1.8 cents per kilowatt-hour) for the first 6,000 megawatts produced by new advanced reactors; and federally funded standby insurance protecting a company building a new plant in the event of unforeseen regulatory delays.

The bill also authorizes almost $3 billion for nuclear energy research, including funding for a new demonstration hydrogen reactor, as well as hydrogen demonstration projects at existing reactors.

The nuclear energy industry has partnered with DOE to design, license and build the next generation of nuclear energy technology. As part of this partnership, companies are testing an improved Nuclear Regulatory Commission process for licensing new nuclear plants. Companies also are testing an early site permit process, which allows a company to gain advance approval for a new reactor site so the location is ready when and if a company decides to build.

Nuclear Energy Is Too Expensive

Charlie Kronick

This selection from Charlie Kronick argues that although nuclear power has been cited as being inexpensive, actual numbers do not support that claim. Building new nuclear plants is expensive, he contends, as is storing nuclear waste. Cleaning up nuclear accidents is also costly, Kronick notes. Constructing the number of nuclear power plants needed to meet future energy needs would be cost-prohibitive, he argues. Charlie Kronick is the director of the Climate Action Network in the United Kingdom.

H oping to reverse its recent decline, the nuclear industry is now presenting itself as a key carbon-free alternative to other forms of electricity generation. Policy-makers, however, should beware: to reduce carbon emissions, nuclear is three to four times more expensive than a mix of renewables, energy-efficiency and co-generation, and retains unacceptably dangerous and insurmountable liabilities.

Problems with Nuclear Power Plants Have Led to Their Decline

Since the late 1980s the nuclear industry has been in steep global decline, particularly in Europe and North America. After the massive accident at Chernobyl, construction of nuclear power stations has reached an almost complete standstill. Within the EU [European Union], seven of the fifteen countries have either phased out nuclear power or never built reactors. All the other countries, only France has one reactor under construction and this is scheduled for completion in 1999. Sweden, the Netherlands and now Germany have phase-out programmes. In others, such as the UK [United Kingdom] and Spain there are no plans for new reactors, making a de-facto phase-out for the nuclear industries there.

Nuclear waste management has proved an intractable problem worldwide: geologically stable and politically acceptable waste repositories are proving elusive. In any case, a waste dump does not make the waste safe: it merely relocates the problem.

Reprocessing nuclear fuel at a site such as the nuclear reprocessing center at Sellafield, England (shown here), is an expensive undertaking.

The expensive and hazardous nuclear fuel reprocessing industry in the UK and France (based at Sellafield and Cap de la Hague) are now threatened by shrinking profitability and increasing restrictions on releases of radioactivity into the environment. Nuclear technology with its complex matrix of unattractive characteristics, has proved "fearsome to manage both socially and politically".

Nuclear Proponents Are Capitalizing on Global Warming

In such an environment, the nuclear industry has unsurprisingly embraced climate change as a sign of a potentially welcome change in its fortunes. The industry is heavily represented at the negotiations of the FCCC [Framework Convention on Climate Control], with 150 officially registered delegates—compared with only 21 registered by the Global Climate Coalition—the principal fossil fuel lobbying group. At Bonn in June 1998 and in Buenos Aires in November 1998, the industry continued to present itself to negotiators, government representatives and commentators as a carbon-free alternative to other forms of electricity generation.

Within its own constituency, the nuclear industry is surprisingly frank in its assessment of the opportunity provided by climate change: the "global climate issue is good for nuclear but the industry needs to build bridges with some environmentalists[!] . . . plants have to be economical; global warming will not justify high cost operation". Yet while the nuclear industry may see the climate issue as "good" news, not all stakeholders have proved open to nuclear industry persuasion. Even the European Union—no hotbed of environmental radicalism—is sceptical about the claims of the industry. EU Energy Commissioner Christos Papoutsis questions the assertions of the nuclear industry while endorsing renewable forms of energy.

Nuclear Power Plants Are Expensive

The basis of the claims made for nuclear by its champions is that it is low in, or even free from carbon emissions. This claim however—which has been extensively questioned in any case—is not adequate to offset its many serious disadvantages.

Nuclear power is very expensive: two decades of experience have shown a huge uncertainty range in the economic costs of nuclear power. Cost escalation pressure comes from a range of sources including high construction costs for new plant, ageing and maintenance problems, as well as growing waste and de-commissioning costs. Unrealistically low utility cost assessments have created huge hidden subsidies to nuclear programmes which are inevitably passed on as costs to ratepayers and taxpayers. Even once built, nuclear facilities are not cheap: depending on their location and the regulatory regime under which they operate, nuclear electricity is more expensive than low carbon fossil fuels such as gas and is even more expensive than genuine renewables like wind and hydro power.

FACTS TO CONSIDER

Nuclear Power Survives on the Public Dole

During atomic energy's half-century of commercial existence, the industry has survived on the public dole, clinging to life supported by subsidy after subsidy. Nuclear has become the most heavily subsidized energy source, from the industry's federally backed insurance limiting utilities' liability to rate payers who absorbed the enormous construction costs through years of high energy prices.

Laura Maggi, *American Prospect*, February 28, 2000.

Five thousand nuclear plants would be needed to displace the 9.4 TW (terawatts) of coal estimated to be necessary in electricity generation in the world by 2025. This is clearly in the realms of fantasy when account is made of the deployment of capital necessary for the task. It would necessitate a new plant starting construction every 2.5 days, even with a favourable six year completion time. On the basis of highly optimistic assumptions concerning capital costs and plant reliability, total electricity generation cost would average $525 billion per year, with the share burdened by developing countries amounting to $170 billion. That share would be for 155 times more nuclear capacity in developing countries compared with today.

In terms of carbon abatement (the cost of reducing CO_2 emissions compared to "business as usual") nuclear energy is also expensive. A mix of renewables, energy efficiency and co-generation is three to four times cheaper than nuclear power for reducing carbon emissions compared to coal-fired power stations.

This 1990s photo shows a nuclear power plant being built. Construction of new nuclear plants has diminished due to safety concerns.

The nuclear industry has not and cannot economically solve the problems of waste and decommissioning: the failure of Nirex in the UK to obtain permission to build the first stages of an underground waste repository for medium-level nuclear waste illuminates the political aspect of this problem. In any policy environment policy, the timescales—literally hundreds of millennia—required for management of nuclear waste underline the impossibility of any such repository ever being "safe" or "sustainable".

Reprocessing of nuclear waste does not eliminate it; it transforms small(er) volumes of spent nuclear fuel into medium- and low-level wastes, plus highly concentrated high-level waste. Both of the major reprocessing plants in Europe—Sellafield in the UK and Cap de la Hague in France—have been responsible for large discharges of dangerous radioactivity into the air and sea.

Nuclear Power Plants Are Inherently Unsafe

Nuclear power is subject to the risk of a major accident. The financial costs of such an accident are difficult to assess, but have been estimated to range from several billion US dollars to several thousand billion US dollars. Costs in human terms are also difficult to assess, but the accident at Chernobyl in 1986 is calculated to have resulted in an increase in thyroid cancers of up to 100 times. Thyroid cancers are seen as early indicators of other, additional, non-fatal cancers, genetic disorders and other radiation-linked diseases that are likely to manifest at a later date.

Even if there could be a total guarantee of no major accidents, all nuclear power stations routinely discharge radioactivity into the surrounding environment. Even if 99-per-cent perfect containment was achieved of the caesium 137 produced by a hundred nuclear power plants, 25 years of operation would still result in caesium 137 contamination equivalent to four Chernobyl accidents.

Civilian nuclear power programmes cannot be separated from the risk of increase in nuclear weapons proliferation. The end of the Cold War has not removed that risk; civil nuclear programmes are the source of more than one thousand tonnes of plutonium, for the most part in the form of spent nuclear fuel. Civil nuclear programmes in countries as diverse as India and the UK produced the plutonium required for their nuclear weapons. Monitoring these stocks of plutonium is extremely difficult; even the International Atomic Energy Authority (IAEA) lacks confidence in its own monitoring system: "the IAEA's verification system cannot physically prevent diversion

A nuclear reprocessing plant like the one shown here reduces the radioactive levels of spent nuclear fuel.

of nuclear materials or the setting up of an undeclared or clandestine nuclear weapons programme."

Nuclear power is not free from carbon emissions, as an analysis of the entire cycle of producing nuclear energy makes clear. Producing nuclear power requires the mining of uranium ore, the enrichment of uranium, as well as the steel, concrete and other materials needed to build a nuclear power station (which is comprised mainly of materials and services derived from fossil fuels). A life cycle analysis of a nuclear plant shows that emissions range up to 60 [grams] [carbon]/KWh [kilowatt/hour]. A typical Pressurised Water Reactor (PWR), such as Sizewell B, operated under UK is responsible for indirect CO_2 emissions of up to 63,000 tonnes per year.

While this may be favourable when compared purely in supply terms with coal, oil or gas, nuclear power suffers when compared with a strategy employing energy-efficiency measures, renewable energy and co-generation.

Nuclear Power Can Benefit the Environment

Patrick Moore

In this selection Patrick Moore discusses the benefits of nuclear power. He asserts that nuclear power's chief benefit is that nuclear facilities do not emit greenhouse gases like fossil fuel plants do. Therefore, he maintains, nuclear energy can help address global warming. In addition to producing affordable, clean energy, nuclear power could also be used to make hydrogen, which can be used as a clean fuel, reducing greenhouse gas emissions even further. Moore was a founder of Greenpeace, but he split with that organization to become chairman and chief scientist of Greenspirit Strategies, an environmental consulting firm. He lives in Vancouver, Canada.

Nuclear energy is the only non-greenhouse-gas-emitting power source that can effectively replace fossil fuels and satisfy global energy demand. Yet it's clear to me that much of the environmental movement—including Greenpeace, the group I co-founded and helped lead for 15 years—has lost its way, caught up in politically correct ideology and stooping to sensationalism to garner support.

As a prime example, Greenpeace and others fail to consider the enormous and obvious benefits of harnessing nuclear power to meet and secure America's growing energy needs. These ben-

Patrick Moore, "An Environmentalist Revisists Nuclear Energy," *Nuclear Policy Outlook*, August, 2005. Reproduced by permission.

efits far outweigh the risks. There is now a great deal of scientific evidence showing nuclear power to be an environmentally sound and safe choice.

Today nuclear energy supplies 20 percent of U.S. electrical energy. The demand for electricity continues to rise and, in the coming decades, may increase by 50 percent over current levels. If nothing is done to revitalize the U.S. nuclear industry, the industry's contribution to meeting U.S. energy demands could drop from 20 percent to 9 percent.

What sources of energy would make up the difference? It is virtually certain that the only technically feasible path is an even greater reliance on fossil fuels. According to the Clean Air Council, annual power plant emissions are responsible for 36 percent of carbon dioxide, 64 percent of sulfur dioxide, 26 percent of nitrogen oxides and 33 percent of mercury emissions. These four pollutants cause significant environmental impact, including acid rain, smog, respiratory illness, mercury contamination, and are the major contributors to greenhouse gas emissions.

Many Environmentalists Support Nuclear Power

Prominent environmental figures like Steward Brand, founder of the Whole Earth Catalog, Gaia theorist James Lovelock and the late Bishop Hugh Montefiore, former Friends of the Earth leader, have stated their strong support for nuclear energy as a practical means of reducing greenhouse gas emissions, while meeting the world's increasing energy demands. I place myself squarely in that category. Indeed, nuclear power is already a proven alternative to fossil fuels.

Nuclear energy prevents the release of 697 million metric tons of carbon dioxide into the air, had this electricity been produced by coal. In fact, the electricity sector's carbon emissions would have been 28 percent higher without nuclear power. A doubling of nuclear energy production would make it possible to reduce significantly total greenhouse gas emissions nationwide.

I also believe there should be a much greater emphasis on renewable energy production. The two most important renewable energy technologies are wind energy, which has great potential, and ground-source heat pumps, known as geothermal or GeoExchange.

As Brand and other forward-thinking environmentalists and scientists have made clear, technology has progressed to the point where activist fear mongering about the safety of nuclear energy bears no resemblance to reality.

Learning from Past Problems

The Chernobyl and Three Mile Island reactors, often raised as examples of nuclear catastrophe by activists, were very different

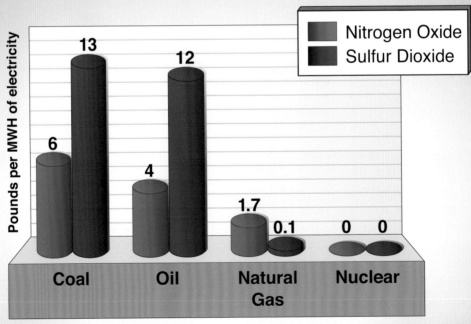

Power Plant Emissions

Power plant emissions only, not including small emissions from mining, transportation and refining or enriching fuel.

"Energy Crisis," Cartoon by Chuck Asay, Copyright © 2004 Creators Syndicate. Used by permission.

from today's rigorously safe nuclear energy technology. Chernobyl was an accident waiting to happen: bad design, shoddy construction, poor maintenance and unprofessional operation all combined to cause the only terrible accident in reactor history. Three Mile Island was a success story in that the radiation from the partially melted core was contained by the concrete containment structure; it did the job it was designed to do.

Today, approximately one-third of the cost of a nuclear reactor is dedicated to safety systems and infrastructure. There are over 100 nuclear reactors in the United States and more than 400 worldwide that are producing electricity every day without serious incident.

The fact that reactors produce nuclear waste is often used to support opposition to them. First, there is no technical obstacle to keeping nuclear waste from entering the environment at harmful levels. Second, this is already being accomplished at hundreds of nuclear power sites around the world. It is simply an issue of secure containment and maintenance. Most important, the spent fuel from reactors still has over 95 percent of its potential energy contained within it. Spent fuel should be stored securely so that in the future we can use this energy productively.

Nuclear reactors produce plutonium that can be extracted and manufactured into nuclear weapons. This is unfortunate but is not in itself justification for eliminating nuclear energy. It appears that the main technologies that have resulted in combat deaths in recent years are machetes, rifles, and car bombs. No one would seriously suggest banning machetes, guns, cars or the fertilizer and diesel that explosives are made from. Nuclear proliferation must be addressed as a separate policy issue from the production of nuclear energy.

Nuclear Energy Offers Other Benefits

Nuclear power offers an important and practical pathway to the proposed "hydrogen economy." Unfortunately there are no hydrogen mines where we can source this element directly. It must be manufactured, from fossil fuels, biomass, or by splitting water into hydrogen and oxygen. Splitting water is the only non-greenhouse gas emitting approach to manufacturing clean hydrogen.

Additionally, nuclear energy could be used to solve another growing crisis: the increasing shortage of fresh water available for human consumption and crop irrigation globally. By using nuclear energy, seawater could be desalinized to satisfy the ever-growing demand for fresh water without the carbon dioxide emissions caused by fossil-fueled power plants.

Nuclear energy—combined with the use of renewable energy sources like wind, geothermal and hydro—remains the only practical, safe and environmentally friendly means of reducing greenhouse gas emissions and addressing energy security. The time for common sense, scientifically sound leadership—and growth—on the nuclear energy issue is now.

Nuclear Power Is Not the Solution to Environmental Problems

Thomas Cochran

Thomas Cochran is the top nuclear physicist for the National Resources Defense Council (NDRC), a national environmental action organization. In this selection he claims that nuclear power is not the answer for limiting greenhouse gas emissions. He cites statistics that show that the United States would need many more nuclear power plants in order to meet rising energy needs, which would result in more radioactive waste needing to be disposed of. Moreover, nuclear power is expensive compared to energy from fossil fuels, thus it is unlikely that nuclear plants would ever replace gas and coal plants.

Over the past year, two of the most hotly contested energy issues of the past half-century have converged on a world-wide scale of global warming and nuclear power. Nuclear reactors generate electricity by splitting atoms, not by burning carbon-based fuel, so the plants themselves don't emit greenhouse gases; this makes them appear to be a good way to curb global warming. China and India are already forging ahead with ambitious plans to expand their fleet of nuclear reactors, and Finland is now building Europe's first new nuclear power plant in 15 years.

Thomas Cochran, "The Nuclear Option," *Onearth*, Spring, 2006, pp. 46–47.
Copyright 2006 Nuclear Energy Institute. Reproduced by permission.

In the United States, where an order for a new nuclear reactor has not been filled in three decades, Congress has granted billions of dollars in subsidies to the nuclear industry for the construction of a handful of new reactors. But behind the debate lies the stark reality that nuclear power is not likely to be the global warming panacea some might hope for. Thomas Cochran, director of NRDC's [National Resources Defense Council] nuclear program and member of the Department of Energy's nuclear energy research advisory committee, explains why.

Expansion Would Be a Problem

NRDC calculated how many nuclear reactors the world would need to build in lieu of new fossil fuel–fired plants to measurably curb the rise in global temperature. It turns out that if we added 700 gigawatts of nuclear capacity—about twice the current global capacity—by 2050, and continued to operate these new plants through the end of the century, it would prevent a global temperature increase of only about 0.36 degree Fahrenheit. Fueling these new facilities would require about 15 new uranium enrichment plants and another 14 . . . geologic repositories to dispose of the spent fuel, which would contain some one million kilograms of plutonium. When separated from the spent fuel, just a few kilograms of this material harbor the explosive potential sufficient to destroy an area the size of lower Manhattan. This hypothetical nuclear-growth scenario is highly unlikely to occur because new nuclear power plants are still uneconomical. But if it did occur, the proliferation and waste problems would likely prove to be intractable.

Nuclear Power Is Expensive

A study done by scientists at the Massachusetts Institute of Technology in 2003 found that electricity produced by a new nuclear power plant in the United States would cost some 60 percent more than energy generated by a coal-fired or natural gas–fired plant. That study assumed moderate natural gas prices of about $4.50 per thousand cubic feet. We've since entered a period of much higher fuel costs—today's natural gas prices are more than twice that—a factor that makes nuclear more economical

Smog obscures this view of a nuclear reactor and factory in China, which plans to build several more reactors.

than the study showed. Still, in the United States, nuclear energy is unlikely to make a meaningful contribution to solving global warming unless fossil fuel prices stay as high as they are today and the cost of electricity from fossil fuel–fired power plants is increased by placing a significant limit on carbon emissions—something the Bush administration and erstwhile nuclear supporters in Congress have, ironically, refused to do.

The Threat of Nuclear Proliferation

Perhaps the most serious of all the problems that would be exacerbated by dramatically increasing global nuclear capacity is the threat of nuclear proliferation. Highly enriched uranium and plutonium are the two types of fuel used in commercial nuclear reactors, but they're also the two principal ingredients in nuclear weapons—and it takes only a few kilograms of these materials to make a

A uranium conversion plant in Tehran, Iran, adds to fears of terrorists acquiring the elements for nuclear weapons.

nuclear bomb. Gas-centrifuge uranium enrichment technology, which is the preferred method used to enrich uranium for commercial reactor fuel outside the United States, can easily be modified, or supplemented in small, secret facilities, to produce highly enriched uranium for weapons. Iran is building a gas-centrifuge facility right now. Moreover, plutonium is a normal by-product of electricity production in conventional reactors. Thus, the same reactors and fuel-processing facilities that are used for energy production can also be used for the manufacture of weapons.

Under current international safeguards, any nation that does not posses nuclear weapons can lawfully acquire nuclear reactors, uranium enrichment plants, and nuclear fuel reprocessing plants, claiming, as do Iran and Japan, that these facilities are solely for peaceful uses. Such nations can also stockpile highly enriched uranium and plutonium—a risk, since the time it would take to convert the materials into a nuclear weapon can be less than the time required for inspectors to detect the diversion and alert the international community.

Nuclear Waste

We need to come up with a safe way to dispose of the highly radioactive spent fuel before we greatly expand existing nuclear power plant capacity. It ranks among the most dangerous materials known; exposure to it causes cancer and birth defects. There is no operational geological repository for spent fuel anywhere in the world. The federal government has spent decades and billions of dollars trying to establish a geologic repository at Nevada's Yucca Mountain, only to learn that leakage from the facility represents a far greater risk to future generations than was believed when the site was selected. The government's response has been to relax the licensing criteria to ensure that the facility receives an operating license. There has been no work on a second repository even though within a few years we'll have generated more waste than even Yucca Mountain could hold.

Safety Issues

While the risk of a catastrophic core meltdown at a reactor in the United States is considered to be much lower today than it was two decades ago, dangerous precursor events still occur. The next serious nuclear accident is most likely to happen in China, India, or Russia, where reactor safety standards are far less stringent.

Nuclear power is the only energy technology currently in use that requires international safeguards intended to prevent the construction of weapons from the fuel. It is also the only technology that produces spent fuel so dangerous that governments must own and dispose of it. In the United States, the nuclear power industry would not be able to survive without federal insurance against catastrophic accidents. So one is right to wonder why, if there are so many problems with the nuclear industry, other countries are deciding to move ahead with plans to expand their nuclear capacity. The answers vary. In Finland the government wants to reduce its dependence on Russian natural gas. In several countries—most notably France, Russia, and China—energy supply technologies are selected by federal bureaucracies or state-owned monopolies rather than in free, fair, and open competition. Even in the United States, President [George W.] Bush and the nuclear industry's supporters in Congress are still trying to tilt the scale in favor of nuclear by offering generous tax credits on future electricity sales from new nuclear power plants, guarantees of federal "cost sharing" during the licensing and construction phases—subsidies in the billions of dollars—and federal construction risk insurance.

Our national electricity needs could be met, while simultaneously reducing greenhouse gas emissions by 70 percent or more, through a combination of increased energy efficiency, wind power, solar power, advanced coal-fired plants with carbon capture and storage, and high-efficiency natural gas turbines. It certainly doesn't make sense to spend tens of billions of federal dollars to subsidize just a few new nuclear plants when we have so many other, more promising options for reducing greenhouse gas emissions. That course of action will simply drain research and development funds from more efficient and more cost-competitive non-nuclear technologies, thereby slowing achievement of meaningful carbon dioxide reductions.

Facts About Nuclear Power

Uranium
- Chemical number: 92
- Chemical symbol: U
- Atomic weight: 238.02891
- Density: 17.3 g/cm³
- Uranium is a heavy metal which is found in rocks throughout the world in low concentrations, typically two to four parts per million. Most natural uranium is composed of two isotopes—U-235 and U-238. U-235 is the isotope that is used to fuel nuclear power plants.
- One enriched uranium fuel pellet, which is less than one inch in diameter, has the energy equivalence of 17,000 cubic feet of natural gas, 1,780 pounds of coal, or 149 gallons of oil.

Comparative Electricity Production Costs per Kilowatt-Hour (2004)

Nuclear energy	1.68 cents
Coal	1.90 cents
Oil	5.39 cents
Gas	5.87 cents

Typical Radiation Exposures (millirems per person per year)

Radon in the air	200.0
Food and water	40.0
Diagnostic X-rays	40.0
Soil and rocks	28.0
Cosmic rays	27.0
Cross-country plane flight	5.0
Water supply	3.0
Nuclear energy	0.1

Reactors in Operation in the United States

- In the United States there are 103 reactors operating in seven states. These reactors provide 782 billion kilowatt-hours of electricity, or 19.4 percent of the total U.S. electrical supply.

Percentage of electricity generated by nuclear power in the states with operating reactors:

Vermont	73.7 percent
South Carolina	54.5 percent
Connecticut	54.4 percent
New Jersey	51.9 percent
Illinois	50.1 percent
New Hampshire	43.0 percent
New York	29.8 percent

Reactors in Operation Worldwide

- Worldwide, 443 reactors in thirty countries provide 16 percent of all power generation. Twenty-seven new reactors are under construction in 2006.

Countries with the largest percentage of electricity from nuclear power (2005):

France	78.5 percent
Lithuania	69.5 percent
Sweden	46.7 percent
Republic of Korea	44.7 percent
Bulgaria	44.1 percent

Containers for Nuclear Waste

- Containers for transporting nuclear waste on average contain three tons of protective shields for every ton of waste transported. Test standards of the Nuclear Regulatory Commission are rigorous. Containers must not leak after a thirty-foot freefall, a forty-inch drop onto a six-inch-diameter steel rod, thirty minutes in a 1,475°F fire, and eight hours under three feet of water. In a separate test, the containers are submerged under fifty feet of water for eight hours.

- Staged accidents have included testing containers placed on a flatbed truck, which was crashed into a solid wall at eighty miles per hour, broadsiding a truck with a 120-ton locomotive traveling at eighty miles per hour, and dropping a container two thousand feet with an impact speed of 238 miles per hour. In all cases the containers remained intact.

Glossary

atomic energy: Energy that is released in nuclear reactions. There are two types of atomic energy. In one the atom's nuclei are broken up into smaller pieces (fission); in the other nuclei are joined together under intense heat (fusion).

breeder reactor: Produces fissionable material, which could be used for fuel by a gas-cooled reactor or a light water reactor. It needs more uranium to operate and is not used commercially.

chain reaction: The process during fission whereby neutrons hit uranium-235 atoms, splitting them apart and freeing more neutrons, which can then bombard more U-235 atoms. The release may be rapid and uncontrolled as is the case with an atomic bomb, or it can be slow and controlled as it is in nuclear power plants.

China syndrome: The fanciful idea that a nuclear reactor could melt down and get so hot that it would bore its way through the earth to China. In fact, the earth would dissipate the heat long before that happened. A movie with the same name was released just days before the Three Mile Island accident in 1979.

containment building: The structure surrounding a nuclear reactor which is designed to contain any release of radioactive material in the event of an accident.

control rod: A tube made of material such as boron that will absorb neutrons. By absorbing neutrons the rod controls the power of the reactor and prevents the neutrons from causing excessive unwanted fission.

core: The central part of the nuclear reactor that contains the fuel rods.

fallout: The spread of radioactive material or gas released into the air.

fission: The splitting of an atomic nucleus resulting in the release of large amounts of energy.

fuel assembly: A cluster of fuel rods. The reactor core is composed of many fuel assemblies.

fuel pellet: A hard ceramic pellet of enriched uranium. A fuel pellet is less than an inch in diameter.

fusion: A reaction in which a heavy, stable nucleus is created by joining two lighter, less stable nuclei. The sun and stars are in effect giant fusion reactors.

gas-cooled reactor (GCR): A reactor that uses gas as a coolant. Typically larger and more expensive than a light water reactor (LWR), GCRs are not competitive with LWRs.

greenhouse gases: Carbon dioxide, sulfur dioxide, and nitrogen oxide. These gases trap heat in the atmosphere and contribute to global warming.

half-life: The time it takes for half of the atoms in a radioactive material to decay and lose their radioactivity. Half-lives can range from a fraction of a second to billions of years.

heavy water: Water that contains heavy hydrogen or deuterium. Heavy water is used in some reactors to slow neutrons.

light water: Ordinary water as opposed to heavy water.

light water reactor (LWR): The reactor most commonly used in the United States. It uses enriched uranium for fuel. Ordinary water circulates through the system and is heated into steam before passing into the steam generator.

Manhattan Project: The top-secret World War II project to develop the atomic bomb.

nuclear waste: Radioactive material that can no longer be used to produce electricity. This material includes spent fuel rods, depleted uranium, and waste from uranium processing. Fuel rods are considered spent when they are no longer capable of sustaining a chain reaction.

uranium: Uranium in nature is generally less than 1 percent fissionable and must be enriched to the 4 percent level before it can be used in a nuclear reactor. The uranium would have to be enriched to the 20 percent fissionable level or more to be used for weapons.

Chronology

1938

Otto Hahn and Fritz Strassman demonstrate nuclear fission by splitting the nucleus of a uranium atom with a neutron.

1942

The top secret Manhattan Project is established in August to develop the nuclear bomb; Enrico Fermi makes the first man-made chain reaction in his laboratory at Stagg Field, University of Chicago.

1945

On July 16 at 5:30 A.M. the world's first nuclear device is exploded at Alamogordo, New Mexico; on August 6 the United States drops an atomic bomb on Hiroshima, Japan, killing seventy to eighty thousand people; on August 9 the United States drops a second bomb on Nagasaki, Japan, killing at least thirty-five thousand people.

1946

President Harry S. Truman signs the McMahan Act on August 1, creating the U.S. Atomic Energy Commission and making nuclear energy a government-owned monopoly.

1953

President Dwight D. Eisenhower delivers his "Atoms for Peace" speech to the General Assembly of the United Nations on December 8; in it, he advocates for the peaceful use of nuclear power.

1954

The world's first nuclear-powered submarine, USS *Nautilus*, is launched at Groton, Connecticut, on January 21 at a cost of $55 million.

1957

The International Atomic Energy Agency is formed in July to promote the peaceful use of atomic energy; underground testing of atomic bombs begins on September 19 near Las Vegas, Nevada;

the first U.S. commercial nuclear power plant at Shippingport, Pennsylvania, begins operating on December 18, providing electricity to Pittsburgh.

1968
The Nuclear Non-Proliferation Treaty is signed by the United States, the Soviet Union, and fifty-nine other countries on July 1.

1975
Congress replaces the Atomic Energy Commission with the Nuclear Regulatory Commission and the Energy Research and Development Authority.

1977
Congress passes legislation on August 4 to create the U.S. Department of Energy, the federal government's twelfth cabinet-level department.

1979
On March 28 a nuclear accident at Reactor 1 at the Three Mile Island power plant near Harrisburg, Pennsylvania, causes the containment building to be flooded; a small amount of radioactive steam is released into the atmosphere.

1983
More electricity in the United States is generated by nuclear power than by natural gas for the first time; seventy-six reactors produce 59,283 megawatts of electricity.

1984
More electricity in the United States is generated by nuclear power than by hydropower for the first time.

1986
On April 26, 1986, the world's worst nuclear disaster occurs at Chernobyl, eighty miles north of Kiev in the Soviet Union; thirty people are killed immediately as a reactor explodes, and 135,000 more are evacuated from the area.

1992
In October Congress passes the Energy Policy Act, creating the United States Enrichment Corporation. The purpose is to improve efficiency of the uranium processing industry.

1994

The United States and Russia sign the Highly Enriched Uranium Purchase Agreement in January. By this agreement, 500 tons of highly enriched uranium is blended to a lower grade of uranium to be used in nuclear power plants in the United States.

1998

The United States Enrichment Corporation is privatized through an initial public offering on July 28. The new company, USEC Inc., remains closely regulated by the government.

2005

President George W. Bush signs the Energy Policy Act on August 8, providing government incentives for electric utilities that build nuclear power plants.

2006

In his February State of the Union address President Bush makes nuclear power a key element in his plan to end "America's addiction to oil."

For Further Reading

Books

Stephen E. Atkins, *Historical Encyclopedia of Atomic Energy*. Westport, CT: Praeger, 2000.

Eric S. Beckjord, *The Future of Nuclear Power: An Interdisciplinary MIT Study*. Massachusetts Institute of Technology Press, 2003.

Pete V. Domenici, *A Brighter Tomorrow: Fulfilling the Promise of Nuclear Power*. Lanham, MD: Rowman & Littlefield, 2004.

Richard L. Garwin and Georges Charpak, *Megawatts and Megatons: The Future of Nuclear Power and Nuclear Weapons*. Chicago: University of Chicago Press, 2002.

Scott W. Heaberlin, *A Case for Nuclear-Generated Electricity: (Or Why I Think Nuclear Power Is Cool and Why It Is Important That You Think So Too)*. Columbus, OH: Batelle, 2004.

Joel Helgerson, *Nuclear Accidents*. New York: Franklin Watts, 1988.

Zhores A. Medvedev, *The Legacy of Chernobyl*. New York: Norton, 1990.

Robert C. Morris, *Nuclear Power: Economic, Medical, and Political Considerations*. New York: Paragon, 2000.

Samuel J. Walker, *Three Mile Island: A Nuclear Crisis in Historical Perspective*. Berkeley, CA: University of California Press, 2004.

Periodicals

Chris Clarke, "New Nukes Is Bad Nukes: Bush's Plan for Your Radioactive Future," *Earth Island Journal*, Summer 2005.

Thomas Cochran, Christopher Paine, Andrew Koehler, and F. David Doty, "Problems with Nuclear Power," *Issues in Science and Technology*, Summer 2005.

Steve Friess, "A New 'Joe Camel'?" *Newsweek*, April 24, 2006.

Fred Guterl, "Another Nuclear Dawn," *Newsweek*, February 6, 2006.

Christopher Helman, Chana R. Schoenberger, and Rob Wherry, "The Silence of the Nuke Protesters," *Forbes*, January 31, 2005.

W. Conard Holton, "Power Surge: Renewed Interest in Nuclear Energy," *Environmental Health Perspectives*, November 2005.

Susan Holtz, "Nuclear Isn't Cheap," *Alternatives Journal*, Summer 2004.

Bob Irvy, "Nuclear Power Heats Up (Again)," *Popular Science*, October 1, 2003.

Barry Kaufer, "Nuclear Safety," *OECD Observer*, December 2004.

Liz Kruesi, "What the Human Body Can Withstand," *Astronomy*, March 2006.

Christian Le Beau, "A Comeback for Nukes?" *Crain's Chicago Business*, September 27, 2004.

Rod Liddle, "Let's Go Nuclear," *Spectator*, August 21, 2004.

David Lochbaum, "Costly and Dangerous," *Mother Earth News*, April/May 2006.

Rod McCullum, "Hope for Yucca Mountain," *Energy*, Fall 2004.

Nuclear Engineering International, "Nuclear: Not So Bad?" March 2004.

Power Economics, "Doubt Looms over Yucca Mountain," May 2004.

———, "To Nuke or Not to Nuke?" September 28, 2004.

Power Engineering International, "When Will Nuclear Add Up?" April 2005.

Sarah Schafer, "China Leaps Ahead," *Newsweek*, February 6, 2006.

Robert N. Schook, Eileen S. Vergino, Neil Joeck, and Ronald F. Lehman, "Atoms for Peace After Fifty Years," *Issues in Science and Technology*, Spring 2004.

Jonas Siegel, "Nuclear Power Comes Home to Roost," *Bulletin of the Atomic Scientists*, March/April 2005.

Suzanna Strangmeier, "Economic Reports Nix Gas and Oil for New Energy Development," *Natural Gas Week*, October 4, 2004.

———, "U.S. Nuclear Options Growing with New Designs," *Natural Gas Weekly*, April 18, 2005.

Joe Truini, "Funds OK'd for Nuclear Waste Recycling Tests," *Waste News*, November 21, 2005.

Nicholas Varchaver, "Nuclear Spring: Even Some Environmentalists Are Learning to Love America's Most Reviled Source of Energy," *Fortune*, January 10, 2005.

Caspar W. Weinberger, "The Quest for Energy—a Decades-Long Debate," *Forbes*, June 6, 2005.

John C. Zink, "Stars Align for Nuclear Power," *Power Engineering*, January 2005.

———, "U.S. Needs Real-World Proof of Nuclear Economics," *Power Engineering*, September 2003.

Karl Zinmeister, "Nuclear Reactions from the Green Movement," *American Enterprise*, January/February 2005.

Web Sites

American Nuclear Society (www.ans.org). The nonprofit American Nuclear Society has over ten thousand members from sixteen hundred corporations, universities, and government organizations. As a scientific and educational organization, its mission is to promote safe applications of nuclear technology and to promote better public awareness of nuclear science.

Greenpeace International (www.greenpeace.org). Greenpeace is a nonprofit environmental organization that operates in forty countries. It is dedicated to eliminating the use of nuclear technology in military and peacetime applications.

International Atomic Energy Agency (www.iaea.org). The International Atomic Energy Agency is known as the "Atoms for Peace" organization. Established in 1957 as an agency within the United Nations, its purpose is to promote the safe and peaceful use of nuclear technology.

Nuclear Energy Institute (www.nei.org). The Nuclear Energy Institute is a trade association whose purpose is to advance policies that promote nuclear energy and technology around the world. It has corporate members in thirteen countries that represent all aspects of the nuclear industry.

Nuclear Regulatory Commission (www.nrc.gov). The Nuclear Regulatory Commission is a federal agency established in 1974 to oversee the civilian use of nuclear energy. Its responsibilities include regulating the use of nuclear materials, protecting public health and safety, and protecting the environment from nuclear hazards.

Sierra Club Nuclear Waste Task Force (www.sierraclub.org). The Sierra Club, a nonprofit conservation and environmental organization, views nuclear waste as one of the major issues facing the world today. Their Web site includes facts, recommendations, links, and policy statements.

U.S. Department of Energy (www.energy.gov). The Department of Energy's overarching mission is to advance the national, economic, and energy security of the United States; to promote scientific and technological innovation in support of that mission; and to ensure the environmental cleanup of the national nuclear weapons complex.

Index

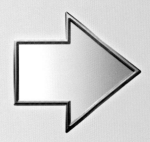

MIT Technology Review (publication), 91–92
Montefiore, Hugh, 103
Moore, Patrick, 91, 102

Nagasaki (Japan), 10, 19
National Academy for Nuclear Training, 52
natural gas, 14, 15, 89
Netherlands, 95
Nevada, 76–77, 80, 84, 111
Nuclear Energy Institute (NEI), 46, 78, 86
nuclear power plants
  are necessary to provide U.S. with electricity needs, 86–87
    con, 112
  are safe, 48–53, 105
    con, 32, 38–45
    standards, 111–12
  construction, 107, 112
    Europe, 94–95
    U.S., 13, 15, 22, 36, 93, 108
  costs, 93, 97, 108, 112
  decommissioning is problem, 99
  early, 12, 19–20
  operation of, 46
  see also radioactive waste; reactor designs; United States, nuclear power plants
nuclear proliferation, 25, 99–100, 110–11
Nuclear Waste Policy Act (1982), 80

oceans, 73–74
oil, 14, 15

Palo Verde nuclear power plant, 58
Papoutsis, Christos, 96
Pennsylvania. See Three Mile Island nuclear power plant
plutonium, 100–101
pollution
  air
    from fossil fuels, 14–15, 103
    nuclear power reduces, 82, 89, 90–93, 102–106
    nuclear power reduction claims are questionable, 94, 96–97, 108
    radiation releases, 12, 40, 41, 51, 99
    reducing without nuclear power, 112
  nuclear power produces carbon, 101
  water from nuclear wastes, 72, 73–74
pressurized water reactors (PWRs), 46–48, 49

Private Ownership of Special Nuclear Materials (1964), 21–22
proliferation, 25, 99–100, 110–11
Public Law 88-489, 21–22

radiation releases
  Germany, 41
  Great Britain, 40
  U.S., 12, 51
radioactive waste
  accidents in repositories, 41
  amount generated, 14
  on site at nuclear power plants, 61, 80–81, 84
  storage in foreign countries, 75
  storage safety is serious problem, 14, 95–96, 99
    con, 14, 80–84, 105–106
  length of time material is toxic, 70, 74–75
  pollution from, 72, 73–74
  U.S. plans, 75–77, 80, 84, 111
  types, 71–74, 77
RBMK reactor design, 42, 44–45
reactor designs
  accidents and, 42–45, 50–51
  are vulnerable to terrorist attacks, 59
  safety standards, 111–12
  types, 46–48, 49
Reagan, Ronald, 14
renewable energy sources, 15, 97, 103–104
research, 17–19, 93
Russia, 112
  see also Soviet Union (former)

safety
  fictional concerns, 12
  nuclear power plants are not safe, 38–45
    are vulnerable to terrorist attacks, 55–56, 57–58, 59–62, 77
    radioactive emissions, 12, 40, 41, 51, 99
    terrorist attacks have occurred, 58–59
  nuclear power plants are safe, 48–53, 56–57, 63–69, 105
  regulations, 36
  standards, 111–12
  storage of waste is serious problem, 14, 95–96, 99
    con, 14, 80–84, 105–106